McDougal Littell
Algebra 2

Larson Boswell Kanold Stiff

Practice Workbook

The Practice Workbook provides additional practice
for every lesson in the textbook. The workbook covers
essential vocabulary, skills, and problem solving. Space
is provided for students to show their work.

McDougal Littell
A DIVISION OF HOUGHTON MIFFLIN COMPANY
Evanston, Illinois • Boston • Dallas

● Contents

Chapter

Name _____ Date _____

 **Practice**
1.1 *For use with pages 2–9*

Graph the numbers on a number line. Decide which number is greater and use the symbol < or > to show the relationship.

1. -5 and -6

2. $-\sqrt{3}$ and 0.75

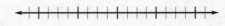

Write the numbers in increasing order.

3. $2, -\dfrac{3}{7}, 0.75, -\dfrac{3}{2}$

4. $3, \sqrt{10}, \dfrac{3}{4}, -1.5$

5. $0, -\sqrt{2}, \sqrt{5}, \dfrac{13}{4}$

Identify the property that the statement illustrates.

6. $(-3)(1) = -3$

7. $5(4 + (-5)) = 5 \cdot 4 + 5 \cdot (-5)$

8. $1 + (3 + 2) = 1 + (2 + 3)$

9. $a + (b + c) = (a + b) + c$

10. $a \cdot \dfrac{1}{a} = 1$

11. $a \cdot b = b \cdot a$

Select and perform an operation to answer the question.

12. What is the sum of -3 and 2?

13. What is the sum of -6 and -2?

14. What is the difference of 4 and 9?

15. What is the difference of -4 and -3?

16. What is the product of -4 and 5?

17. What is the product of -6 and -3?

18. What is the quotient of 49 and -7?

19. What is the quotient of -21 and $-\dfrac{7}{3}$?

LESSON 1.1	**Practice** continued

For use with pages 2–9

Give the answer with the appropriate unit of measure.

20. $-5\frac{1}{4}$ inches $- 2\frac{2}{3}$ inches

21. $-3\frac{1}{3}$ miles $+ 1\frac{2}{3}$ miles

22. Gas Mileage A car can travel 25 miles per gallon of gas. The gas tank contains 9 gallons. How far can the car travel without refueling?

23. Touchdown A football team scored 24 of their 28 points from touchdowns. A touchdown is worth 6 points. How many touchdowns did the team score?

24. Birthday Cake Ten classmates are going to share a birthday cake after school. The rectangular birthday cake is 5 pieces long and 4 pieces wide. Each person eats the same number of pieces. How many pieces does each person eat?

25. Mile Run Jim runs one mile by running four laps around the track. The times in seconds for each lap are shown in the table. What is his total mile time in minutes and seconds? What is his average lap time in seconds?

Lap	1	2	3	4
Time (sec)	91	103	106	98

Name _____ Date _____

Write the expression using exponents.

1. $a \cdot a \cdot a$

2. $(-7) \cdot (-7) \cdot (-7) \cdot (-7)$

3. $(-x)(-x)(-x)(-x)(-x)$

4. $(2x \cdot 2x \cdot 2x) + 5$

5. $(3a \cdot 3a) - (b \cdot b \cdot b \cdot b)$

6. 2 to the nth power

Evaluate the expression.

7. $(-4)^2$

8. -2^4

9. $3 - (4 - 2) \cdot 5$

10. $1 + (5^2 - 10) \div 5$

11. $(6 - 5)^3 + 14 \div (2 + 5)$

12. $24 - (1 + 1)^4 \div 4$

Evaluate the expression for the given value of *x*.

13. $x(x - 3)$ when $x = 7$

14. $3x - 0.5(x - 2x)$ when $x = 4$

15. $3x^2 - 2x$ when $x = -2$

16. $2x^2 \div (4 - 2x) + 2$ when $x = 4$

17. $35 - \frac{2}{3}x^2 \div x$ when $x = 9$

18. $7 - x^3\left(\frac{1}{2x}\right)$ when $x = -2$

Practice *continued*
For use with pages 10–17

Evaluate the expression for the given values of *x* and *y*.

19. $x^2 + 2y^2$ when $x = 3, y = 2$

20. $-3x^2 + (3y)^4$ when $x = -5, y = 1$

21. $\dfrac{3x + y - 1}{2x - y}$ when $x = 3, y = 4$

22. $\dfrac{(2x - 2)^3}{-y^3 - 3}$ when $x = 2, y = -2$

Write an expression for the area of the figure. Evaluate the expression for the given values of the variables.

23. $x = 3, y = 3$

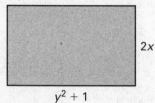

$2x$

$y^2 + 1$

24. $x = 2, y = 5$

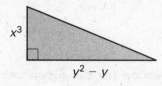

x^3

$y^2 - y$

25. Photography Studio A photography studio advertises a session with a sitting fee of $8.95 per person. The standard package of pictures costs $29.95. Write an expression that gives the total cost of a session plus the purchase of one standard package. Evaluate the expression if a family of four purchases this package.

26. Books You want to buy either a paperback or hard covered book as a gift for five friends. Paperbacks cost $6.95 each and hard covered books cost $24.99 each. Write and simplify an expression for the total amount you spend if x of the books are paperback. Evaluate the expression if three of your friends get a paperback.

Name _____   Date _____

Solve the equation. Check your solution.

1. $x - 9 = 12$

2. $3x - 2 = 16$

3. $3 - x = 2$

4. $-4 = x - 1$

5. $3 = 2 + x$

6. $-14 + 2x = 6$

7. $6x = 24$

8. $-4x = -14$

9. $\frac{3}{2}x + 1 = 13$

10. $\frac{2}{5}x + 10 = 0$

11. $\frac{4}{3}x + 2 = 6$

12. $x + 6 = 3(5 - x)$

13. $x + \frac{3}{2} = \frac{3}{4}\left(x - \frac{1}{2}\right)$

14. $3(x - 2) = 2(2x - 3)$

15. $x + \frac{3}{5} = \frac{7}{5}(x + 1)$

16. $\frac{1}{2}(14x + 2) = 3(2 - 3x)$

17. $5x = \frac{4}{5}(5x - 2)$

18. $x + 6 = 3(3 - x)$

19. $\frac{5}{4}(4x + 2) = 3$

20. $27 - 2x = 2(x + 1)$

21. $x + 4 = 2x - 8\left(\frac{1}{4}x - \frac{1}{4}\right)$

LESSON 1.3 **Practice** *continued*
For use with pages 18–25

22. **Perimeter** The perimeter of the rectangle below is 78 feet. Find its dimensions.

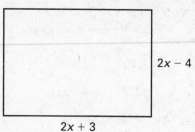

$2x - 4$

$2x + 3$

23. **Movie Tickets** A movie ticket costs $6.50. You have $35.00 to buy tickets and popcorn for four people. How much money is left to buy popcorn after the tickets are paid for?

24. **Pay Rate** You need to earn $475 per week to afford the new car you want to purchase. Your work week is 45 hours. You get 1.5 times the regular hourly rate for overtime (anything over 40 hours). How much does your hourly rate need to be?

25. **Car Bill** The bill for your automobile repairs was $265.74. The cost for labor was $52.00 per hour. The cost for materials was $135.74. How many hours did the mechanic work on your automobile?

26. **Road Trip** On Friday, you drove 145 miles to stay at your grandmother's house. On Sunday, you returned home and calculated that the round trip travel time was 5 hours. What was your average speed?

LESSON 1.4 **Practice**
For use with pages 26–32

Substitute the given value of *x* into the equation. Then solve the equation for *y*.

1. $7x - 3y = 6; x = 3$

2. $6x + 5y = -7; x = -2$

3. $xy = 12 + 3x; x = 4$

4. $\frac{2}{3}x = 2y - \frac{2}{5}; x = -9$

5. $\frac{2}{3}y + \frac{1}{2}x = 1; x = 12$

6. $x - 2y = 3xy + 1; x = -2$

Solve the equation for *y*. Then find the value of *y* for the given value of *x*.

7. $3x - 6y = 6; x = 2$

8. $-2x + 2 = 5y - 1; x = 5$

9. $2xy + 1 = xy + 3; x = 2$

10. $\frac{1}{2}x - y = \frac{3}{2}x - 3; x = 7$

11. $\frac{3}{4}x + \frac{4}{7}y = \frac{5}{4}x - 1; x = 8$

12. $\frac{3}{5}y - 4x = 3 - 2y; x = 9$

Solve the formula for the indicated variable.

13. *Fahrenheit to Celsius*

Solve for F: $C = \frac{5}{9}(F - 32)$

14. *Perimeter of a Parallelogram*

Solve for b: $P = 2b + 2s$

15. *Perimeter of a Triangle*

Solve for c: $P = a + b + c$

16. *Area of a Rhombus*

Solve for d_1: $A = \frac{1}{2}d_1 d_2$

Algebra 2
Chapter 1 Practice Workbook   **7**

Practice *continued*
For use with pages 26–32

17. *Area of a Trapezoid*

Solve for b_1: $A = \frac{1}{2}(b_1 + b_2)h$

18. *Volume of a Right Circular Cylinder*

Solve for h: $V = \pi r^2 h$

19. *Lateral Surface Area of a Right Circular Cylinder*

Solve for h: $S = 2\pi rh$

20. *Volume of a Right Circular Cone*

Solve for h: $V = \frac{\pi r^2 h}{3}$

Solve the formula for the indicated variable. Then use the given information to find the value of the variable. Include units of measure in the answer.

21. *Area of a Parallelogram*

Solve for h: $A = bh$

Find h when $A = 81$ cm^2 and $b = 9$ cm.

22. *Celsius to Fahrenheit*

Solve for C: $F = \frac{9}{5}C + 32$

Find C when $F = 77°$F.

Basketball A regulation size basketball has a volume of 455.9 cubic inches. Use this information to answer the following questions. Approximate your answers to the nearest tenth.

23. The formula for the volume of a sphere is $V = \frac{4}{3}\pi r^3$. What is the radius of the basketball?

24. What is the diameter of the basketball?

25. The formula for the circumference of the basketball is $C = 2\pi r$. If the circumference of a basketball is 29 inches, is it a regulation size basketball?

Algebra 2
Chapter 1 Practice Workbook

Name _____ Date _____

Use the formula $d = rt$ for distance traveled to solve for the missing variable.

1. $d =$ __?__ , $r = 55$ mi/h, $t = 3$ h

2. $d = 240$ mi, $r = 60$ mi/h, $t =$ __?__

3. $d = 552$ mi, $r =$ __?__ , $t = 8$ h

4. $d = 247.5$ mi, $r = 45$ mi/h, $t =$ __?__

Use the formula $A = bh$ for the area of a parallelogram to solve for the missing variable.

5. $A =$ __?__ , $b = 6$ ft, $h = 3$ ft

6. $A = 34$ ft^2, $b =$ __?__ , $h = 4$ ft

7. $A = 175$ m^2, $b = 25$ m, $h =$ __?__

8. $A =$ __?__ , $b = 23$ cm, $h = 15$ cm

Look for a pattern in the table. Then write an equation that represents the table.

9.

x	0	1	2	3
y	5	10	15	20

10.

x	0	1	2	3
y	22	25	28	31

11.

x	0	1	2	3
y	17	16	15	14

12.

x	0	1	2	3
y	89	82	75	68

Practice *continued*
For use with pages 34–40

13. **Fastest Solar Powered Vehicle** The highest speed reached by a solar powered vehicle is 48.71 miles per hour. This record was set by a car called Sunraycer on June 24, 1988 in Mesa, Arizona. How far could Sunraycer travel in 2.5 hours at this speed?

14. **Cable Bill** Your local cable company charges $29.99 per month for basic cable service. Premium channels are available for a surcharge of $5.95 per channel. You have $70 per month budgeted for cable. How many premium channels can you purchase?

15. **Sharing the Drive** You and a friend take turns driving on a 450 mile trip. Your friend drives for 3.5 hours at an average speed of 60 miles per hour. What must your average speed be for the remainder of the trip if you want to reach your hotel in 4 more hours?

16. **Parking Lot** A five gallon bucket of tar can seal 3500 square feet of blacktop. If a parking lot is 15,000 square feet, how many buckets of tar must be purchased in order to seal it?

Practice
LESSON 1.6
For use with pages 41–47

Graph the solution of the inequality.

1. $0 < x < 3$

2. $x \leq -2$ or $x > 1$

Solve the inequality.

3. $x - 5 > 9$

4. $4x \leq 48$

5. $-3 < 7 + 2x$

6. $3x \leq 8 + x$

7. $7x + 3 > 10$

8. $\frac{1}{4}x - 2 < -1$

9. $-x + 4 \geq -2$

10. $5 - 5x \leq 10$

11. $-3x + 7 < -8$

12. $4 < 3 - x$

13. $-3x + 6 \leq 6$

14. $x + 8 \leq 2x - 2$

15. $-3 < x - 3 < 0$

16. $2 \leq x + 3 \leq 5$

17. $x + 2 \leq -1$ or $x - 2 \geq 1$

18. $x - 3 < -4$ or $x - 1 > 5$

19. $3 \leq \frac{1}{3}x - 2 \leq 4$

20. $2(x + 3) > -4$

Name _____   Date _____

Solve the inequality and then graph the solution.

21. $2 - x > 3x + 10$

22. $3(x + 2) \geq 15$

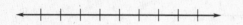

23. **Population of Hawaii** From 2000 to 2003, Hawaii's population grew approximately by 3.8% from 1,211,537 to 1,257,608. Write an inequality that represents the number of people living in Hawaii during this time period.

24. **NBA** The all time leading scorer in NBA history is Kareem Abdul-Jabbar with 38,387 points. The tenth player on this list is John Havlicek with 26,395 points. Write an inequality that represents the range of points scored by the top ten all time leading scorers in NBA history.

25. **Speed Limit** On some sections of the German Autobahn there are no speed limits. Write an inequality that represents the various distances that you could travel in 2.5 hours if your maximum speed was 135 miles per hour during this time period. Solve the inequality.

26. **Exam Grades** The grades for a course are based on 5 exams and 1 final exam. All six of these tests are worth 100 points. To receive an A in the course, you must earn at least 552 points. Your grades on the 5 exams are as follows: 88, 96, 93, 91, and 89. Write an inequality that represents the various grades you can earn on the final exam and still get an A. Solve the inequality.

Name _____   Date _____

Decide whether the number is a solution of the equation.

1. $|2x + 3| = 7; 2$

2. $|3x - 5| = 2; -1$

3. $|2x - 7| = 3; 2$

4. $|4 - 3x| = 10; 2$

5. $\left|\frac{1}{3}x + 3\right| = 6; -9$

6. $\left|2 - \frac{1}{2}x\right| = 5; -6$

Solve the equation.

7. $|x - 3| = 5$

8. $|2x + 6| = 12$

9. $|3x - 3| = 8$

10. $|1 - 2x| = 9$

11. $\left|\frac{2}{3}x + 2\right| = 0$

12. $|9x - 2| = 7$

13. $|2x - 3| = 3$

14. $\left|1 - \frac{1}{5}x\right| = 3$

15. $|5 - 6x| = 7$

| LESSON | **Practice** continued |
| 1.7 | For use with pages 50–58 |

Solve the inequality.

16. $|x - 3| < 8$ 17. $|2x - 3| \geq 5$ 18. $|3 - x| \leq 3$

19. $|x + 7| > 3$ 20. $|4x - 7| < 9$ 21. $|4 - x| \leq 8$

22. $\left|\frac{1}{3}x + 4\right| > 1$ 23. $\left|4 - \frac{1}{2}x\right| \leq 6$ 24. $|2 - 3x| \geq \frac{2}{3}$

25. **Golfing** You plan on going golfing this weekend with a friend. You can either go to your favorite course which is 14 miles north of your house or to your friend's favorite course which is 14 miles south of your house. Write an absolute value inequality that represents all the distances you may be from your house.

26. **Garter Snake** The garter snake is a common species in North America. There are various subspecies and coloration schemes depending on the geographical location. Typical adult garter snakes range in length from 46 to 130 centimeters. Write an absolute value inequality that represents the range of lengths of adult garter snakes.

27. **Homework** On a slow weekday, you spend at least two hours on homework. On a busy weekday, you spend as much as five hours on homework. Write an absolute value inequality that represents the number of hours you spend doing homework on a typical weekday.

28. **African Elephant** The African elephant is the heaviest land animal on the planet. Their mass varies from 3600 to 6000 kilograms. Write an absolute value inequality that represents the mass range of the African elephant.

LESSON 2.1 Practice
For use with pages 72–79

Identify the domain and range of the given relation. Then tell whether the relation is a function.

1. $(0, 3), (1, 1), (2, 2), (3, 4), (4, 2)$

2. $(-2, -3), (-1, -1), (0, 1), (0, 3), (1, 5)$

Use the vertical line test to determine whether the relation is a function.

3.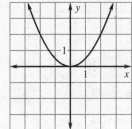

4.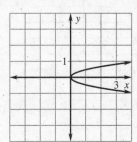

5.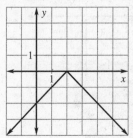

Graph the equation.

6. $y = 3x + 2$

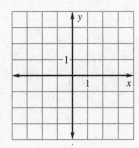

7. $y = -2x - 2$

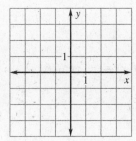

8. $y = -x$

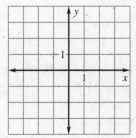

LESSON 2.1

Practice *continued*
For use with pages 72–79

9. $y = -x + 3$

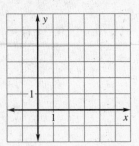

10. $y = \frac{1}{2}x + 2$

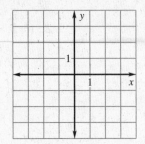

11. $y = 2x - 5$

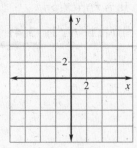

12. $y = x + 2$

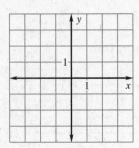

13. $y = -1$

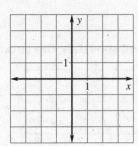

14. $y = -\frac{1}{4}x - 1$

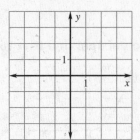

Tell whether the function is linear. Then evaluate the function for the given value of *x*.

15. $f(x) = x + 5; f(-2)$

16. $f(x) = x^2 + x - 2; f(1)$

17. $f(x) = 3 - 3x; f(2)$

18. $f(x) = |x + 2|; f(-4)$

19. $f(x) = \frac{2}{x - 2}; f(6)$

20. $f(x) = \frac{2}{3}x - 5; f(9)$

Copyright © by McDougal Littell, a division of Houghton Mifflin Company.

LESSON 2.1 **Practice** *continued*
For use with pages 72–79

In Exercises 21–23, use the following information.

PGA Money List The table below shows the top five players on the 2005 PGA Tour money list through June 5th along with the number of wins for each player.

Player	Vijay Singh	Phil Mickelson	Tiger Woods	David Toms	Kenny Perry
Wins, x	3	3	3	1	2
Dollars, y (in millions)	5.3	4.2	4.1	3.3	2.5

21. What is the domain of the relation?

22. What is the range of the relation?

23. Is the amount of money earned a function of the number of wins?

In Exercises 24–26, use the following information.

Furniture Assembly At the beginning of your 8 hour shift, there were 42 units of furniture that needed assembled. The number of units n that still need to be assembled during your shift can be modeled by $n(t) = -3t + 42$ where t is the time in hours.

24. Graph the model.

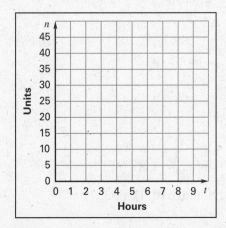

25. What is a reasonable domain and range of the model?

26. How many units still need to be assembled after you have worked 5 hours of your shift?

LESSON 2.2 **Practice**
For use with pages 82–88

Find the slope of the line passing through the given points.

1. $(2, 1), (6, 9)$

2. $(1, 1), (2, -5)$

3. $(-3, 2), (6, -1)$

4. $(3, -2), (-1, 7)$

5. $(0, -5), (-2, -9)$

6. $\left(\frac{1}{3}, \frac{1}{2}\right), \left(\frac{5}{3}, \frac{5}{2}\right)$

Tell which line is steeper.

7. Line 1: through $(-2, 2), (4, 3)$

   Line 2: through $(2, 3), (6, 4)$

8. Line 1: through $(5, 2), (7, 12)$

   Line 2: through $(-3, -1), (-2, 5)$

9. Line 1: through $(1, 1), (3, 0)$

   Line 2: through $(4, 2), (8, -2)$

10. Line 1: through $(3, 8), (6, 17)$

    Line 2: through $(0, 1), (-3, 7)$

LESSON 2.2 **Practice** *continued*
For use with pages 82–88

Find the slope of the line passing through the given points. Then tell whether the line *rises, falls, is horizontal*, or *is vertical*.

11. $(-2, 4), (2, 5)$

12. $(3, 1), (3, -2)$

13. $(8, 15), (12, -1)$

14. $(5, -2), (2, -2)$

15. $(9, -3), (-6, 4)$

16. $(4, 5), (21, 5)$

Tell whether the lines are *parallel, perpendicular*, or *neither*.

17. Line 1: through $(-6, 2), (3, 5)$

Line 2: through $(4, 1), (1, 0)$

18. Line 1: through $(7, 3), (8, 7)$

Line 2: through $(-5, -4), (-1, -5)$

19. Line 1: through $(5, 2), (1, -7)$

Line 2: through $(-1, 3), (9, -1)$

20. Line 1: through $(5, 9), (7, 13)$

Line 2: through $(0, 2), (4, 10)$

21. **Fuel Efficiency** On Friday, you left for a weekend camping trip with 110 miles on the odometer and 14.5 gallons of gas in the tank of your car. When you returned on Sunday, the odometer read 299 miles and you still had 7.5 gallons of gas left. What was the fuel efficiency of your car on this trip?

22. **Production Rate** When you started your shift at 7:00 A.M., 120 steel valves had already been machined and were ready for assembly. At 3:00 P.M., your shift ended and 424 steel valves were now completed and ready for assembly. The target production rate is 36 steel valves per hour. What was the production rate for your shift? Would your supervisor be satisfied with the work pace?

LESSON 2.3 Practice
For use with pages 89–97

Find the slope and *y*-intercept of the line.

1. $y = 7x + 8$

2. $y = -13x$

3. $2x + y - 2 = 0$

4. $4x + 2y - 5 = 0$

5. $5x - y + 2 = 0$

6. $-3x + 2y - 4 = 0$

Find the *x*- and *y*-intercepts of the line with the given equation.

7. $y = 4x - 1$

8. $y = -x - 4$

9. $y = -\frac{1}{2}x + 2$

10. $y = \frac{3}{2}x + 1$

11. $y = \frac{4}{3}x - 2$

12. $y = -\frac{1}{3}x - 3$

13. $x - y - 3 = 0$

14. $2x - 3y + 6 = 0$

15. $-7x - 14y - 5 = 0$

16. $4x - 2y = 1$

17. $6x + 4y = -5$

18. $-3x + y = -8$

LESSON 2.3 **Practice** *continued*
For use with pages 89–97

Graph the equation.

19. $y = 3x + 3$

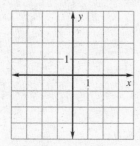

20. $y = -2x - 6$

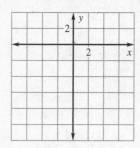

21. $x - 2y + 2 = 0$

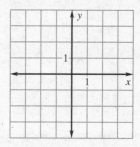

22. $5x + 2y + 6 = 0$

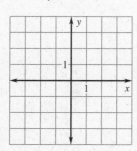

23. $-6x + 3y - 18 = 0$

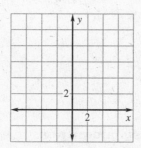

24. $12x - 8y = -24$

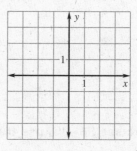

25. $2x + y = -3$

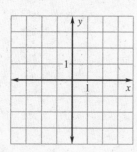

26. $3x + y = 0$

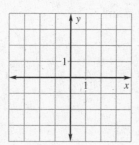

27. $-5x + 3y - 15 = 0$

28. $2y = -5x - 4$

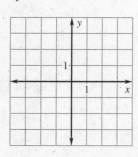

29. $-3y = 6x$

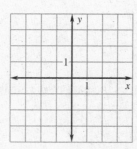

30. $6y - 18 = 0$

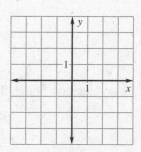

Practice *continued*
For use with pages 89–97

31. Hot Dogs and Hamburgers The caterer for your class picnic charges $1 for each hot dog and $2 for each hamburger. You have $48 to spend. Write a model that shows the different numbers of hot dogs and hamburgers that you could purchase.

32. Commission A car salesperson earns 2% on used car sales and 6% on new car sales. The salesperson wants to earn a $7000 commission this month. Write a model that shows the different sales amounts of used and new cars that can be sold to reach the target commission.

In Exercises 33–35, use the following information.

Airplane Landing An airplane's altitude is 100 feet as it is descending for a landing on a runway whose touchdown point is 5000 feet away. Let the x-axis represent the distance on the ground and the y-axis represent the airplane's altitude.

33. What is the slope of the airplane's descent?

34. What is the y-intercept of the airplane's descent?

35. Write an equation of the line that follows the path of the airplane's descent.

Practice

For use with pages 98–104

Write an equation of the line that has the given slope and y-intercept.

1. $m = 3, b = -4$ **2.** $m = -4, b = 0$ **3.** $m = 0, b = -5$

Write an equation of the line that passes through the given point and has the given slope.

4. $(4, 3), m = 1$ **5.** $(-1, 1), m = -2$ **6.** $(12, 4), m = 0$

7. $\left(\dfrac{2}{3}, 1\right), m = -3$ **8.** $\left(-2, \dfrac{1}{2}\right), m = 8$ **9.** $\left(\dfrac{3}{5}, 0\right), m = -5$

Write an equation of the line that passes through the given point and satisfies the given condition.

10. $(-2, 3)$; parallel to $y = 4x - 3$ **11.** $(3, 7)$; parallel to $y = -3x + 6$

12. $(-1, -4)$; perpendicular to $y = 2x + 5$ **13.** $(6, -2)$; perpendicular to $y = -5x - 7$

Name _____ Date _____

Write an equation of the line that passes through the given points.

14. $(3, 4), (0, 3)$

15. $(-3, -3), (2, 1)$

16. $(-5, -4), (0, 11)$

17. $(1, -4), (-2, 6)$

18. $(2, 8), (5, 2)$

19. $(-8, -3), (7, 0)$

Write an equation of the line.

20.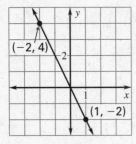

21.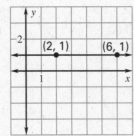

22.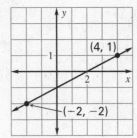

23. Video Store The membership to your local video store is $10 per year and the DVD rental rate is $3.95 per DVD. Write an equation that models the total amount of money you will spend on DVD rentals this year.

In Exercises 24 and 25, use the following information.

Postal Rates The price for U.S. postage stamps has increased over the years. Since 1975, the price has increased from $.13 to $.37 in 2005 at a rate that is approximately linear.

24. Write a linear model for the price of stamps during this time period. Let p represent the price and t represent the number of years since 1975.

25. What would you expect the price of a stamp to be in 2015?

Name _____ Date _____

Write and graph a direct variation equation that has the given ordered pair as a solution.

1. $(5, 10)$

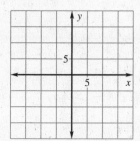

2. $(-6, 3)$

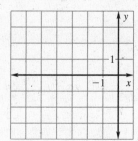

3. $(-5, -2)$

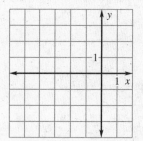

The variables x and y vary directly. Write an equation that relates x and y. Then find y when $x = 3$.

4. $x = 6, y = -8$

5. $x = -4, y = -16$

6. $x = 2, y = 14$

7. $x = -4, y = -20$

8. $x = 12, y = -4$

9. $x = 7, y = 4$

10. $x = -6, y = -1$

11. $x = -10, y = -15$

12. $x = 10, y = 4$

LESSON	**Practice** continued
2.5	*For use with pages 107–111*

Tell whether the equation represents direct variation. If it does, give the constant of variation.

13. $y = -3x$

14. $y + 2 = 8x$

15. $2y - 6 = 0$

16. $6x + y = 2$

17. $-6x + 4y = 0$

18. $3y = \dfrac{9}{2}x$

Tell whether the data in the table show a direct variation. If so, write an equation relating x and y.

19.

x	−2	−1	0	1	2
y	4	3	2	1	0

20.

x	−3	−1	1	3	5
y	−2	$-\dfrac{2}{3}$	$\dfrac{2}{3}$	2	$\dfrac{10}{3}$

21. Reading The number of pages p a student can read varies directly with the amount of time t in minutes spent reading. The student can read 90 pages in 60 minutes. Write an equation that relates p and t. Predict the number of pages the student can read if 90 minutes is spent reading.

22. Movies The cost c of going to the movies varies directly with the number n of people attending. A group of four paid $14 to go to the movies on Friday. Write an equation that relates c and n. How much would it cost for 7 people to go to the movies?

LESSON 2.6 **Practice**
For use with pages 112–120

Draw a scatter plot of the data. Tell whether the data have a *positive correlation,* a *negative correlation,* or *approximately no correlation.*

1.

x	0	0.5	1.25	2.75	3
y	−3.5	−2	−0.75	1.25	2.5
x	3.5	4.25	4.75	5.25	6
y	3.25	5.5	7	8.25	9.5

2.

x	−1.5	−1	−0.75	0	1.5
y	−5.25	−2.5	4	5.75	−1.75
x	2	2.25	3	3.5	4
y	−3	4.25	5.5	1.75	−1.25

Approximate the best-fitting line for the data.

3.
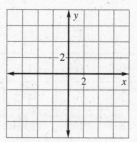

4.
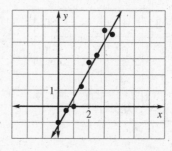

LESSON 2.6 **Practice** *continued*
For use with pages 112–120

Draw a scatter plot of the data. Approximate the best-fitting line for the data.

5.

x	0.5	1	1.5	2	2.5
y	−2.25	−2.75	−1.7	−0.5	0
x	3	3.5	4	4.5	5
y	−0.6	1.2	1.9	2.5	2.3

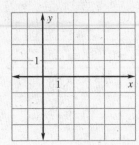

6.

x	−4	−3	−2	−1	0
y	2	−0.5	0	−1.5	−4.2
x	1	2	3	4	
y	−5.8	−8.8	−9.5	−11.4	

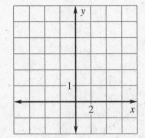

7.

x	−4	−3	−2	−1	0
y	2.5	3	1.5	2	1
x	1	2	3	4	
y	2	3.5	0.5	2.5	

In Exercises 8–10, use the following information.

Softball The table shows the number of adult softball teams for the years 1999 to 2003.

Year	1999	2000	2001	2002	2003
Number of teams (in thousands)	163	155	149	143	119

8. Draw a scatter plot for the data. Let *t* represent the number of years since 1999.

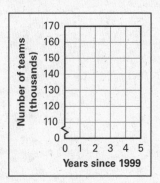

9. Using a graphing calculator, approximate the best-fitting line for the data.

10. Using this model, predict the number of adult softball teams in 2010.

LESSON 2.7 **Practice**
For use with pages 121–129

For the function (a) tell whether the graph *opens up* or *down*, (b) identify the vertex, and (c) tell whether the function is *wider*, *narrower*, or the *same width* as the graph of $y = |x|$.

1. $y = -|x + 1|$

2. $f(x) = 7|x - 3| - 4$

3. $y = -4|x + 2| + 2$

4. $f(x) = 2|x + 2| + 8$

5. $y = -\frac{2}{3}|x + 1|$

6. $f(x) = -|x| - 5$

7. $y = \frac{5}{2}|x + 9| - 1$

8. $f(x) = \frac{7}{8}|x + 3| - 9$

9. $y = -\frac{7}{5}|x - 1| + 1$

Graph the function.

10. $y = |x| - 3$

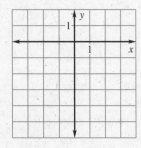

11. $f(x) = |x - 3|$

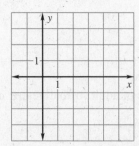

12. $y = |x + 2| + 1$

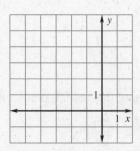

Algebra 2

LESSON 2.7 **Practice** continued
For use with pages 121–129

13. $y = 2|x + 1| - 1$

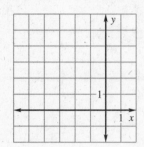

14. $f(x) = \frac{1}{2}|x - 3| + 2$

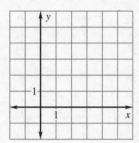

15. $y = -\frac{3}{2}|x - 4| + 2$

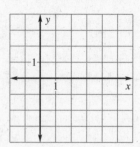

Write an equation of the graph shown.

16.

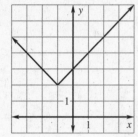

17.

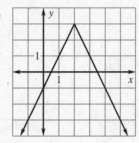

18.

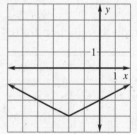

Let $f(x) = x + 2$. Sketch $f(x)$ and then sketch the function y given by the transformation to $f(x)$.

19. $y = f(x) + 1$

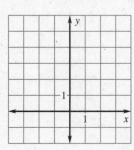

20. $y = f(x - 2)$

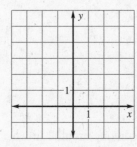

21. $y = -2f(x)$

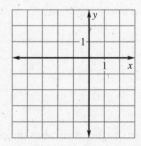

LESSON 2.7 **Practice** *continued*
For use with pages 121–129

22. $y = \frac{1}{4}f(x)$

23. $y = 3f(x + 2) - 1$

24. $y = -f(x - 1) + 3$

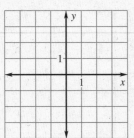

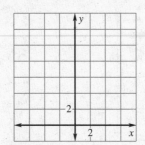

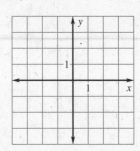

In Exercises 25–27, use the following information.

Speedboats The number of boats B a boat dealer sells in each month of the year can be modeled by the function $B = -15\,|t - 5| + 120$ where t is the time in months and $t = 1$ represents January.

25. Graph the function for $0 \le t \le 12$.

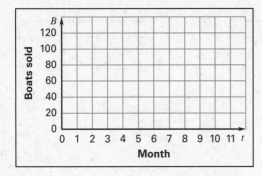

26. What is the maximum number of sales in one month? In what month is the maximum reached?

27. What is the minimum number of sales in one month? In what month is the minimum reached?

Name _____   Date _____

Practice
For use with pages 132–138

Tell whether the given ordered pairs are solutions of the inequality.

1. $x - y < 4$; $(5, 4)$, $(-1, -4)$

2. $2x + 3y \le -3$; $(0, -1)$, $(-3, 2)$

3. $4x - 2y > 5$; $(5, 8)$, $(-1, -4)$

4. $8y - 2x \ge 15$; $(1, 2)$, $(3, 3)$

5. $2y < 5x + 10$; $(-2, -1)$, $(-1, 2)$

6. $10x \ge 14 - 8y$; $(2, 4)$, $(4, -3)$

Graph the inequality in a coordinate plane.

7. $x > 2$

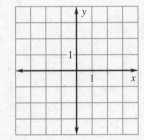

8. $x \le -1$

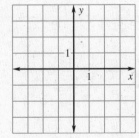

9. $2x \le 8$

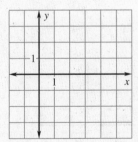

LESSON
2.8

Practice *continued*
For use with pages 132–138

10. $y \geq -2$

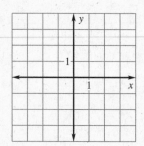

11. $y < 3$

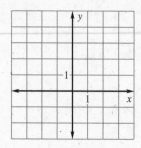

12. $\frac{1}{4}y \leq 1$

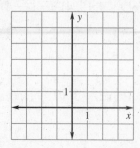

13. $y < 2x - 1$

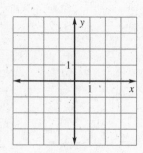

14. $y \geq \frac{1}{2}x + 2$

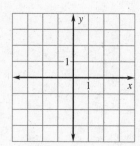

15. $3x + y > -3$

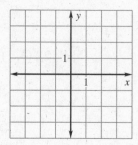

16. $x + 3y \leq 6$

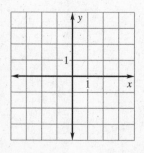

17. $x - 3y > -3$

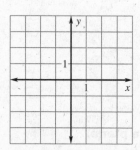

18. $-6x - 2y \leq 4$

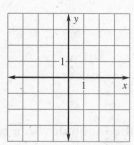

19. $y > 4|x| - 3$

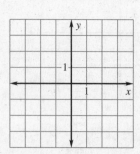

20. $y \geq |x + 1| + 2$

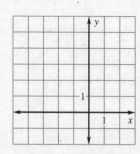

21. $y \leq -\frac{1}{2}|x - 2| + 4$

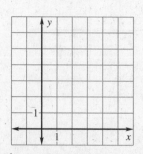

Algebra 2

LESSON 2.8

Practice *continued*
For use with pages 132–138

In Exercises 22–24, use the following information.

Summer Job You offer to mow your neighbors' lawns for $20 or to wash their cars for $10. Your goal is to earn at least $1500 this summer.

22. Write and graph an inequality that represents the possible number of lawns you would have to mow x and cars you would have to wash y in order to reach your goal.

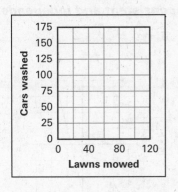

23. What are the coordinates of mowing 50 lawns and washing 65 cars?

24. Is the point in Exercise 23 a solution of the inequality?

In Exercises 25–27, use the following information.

Music Lessons Your parents have budgeted $550 for you to take music lessons on the piano for $25 and on the saxophone for $20.

25. Write and graph an inequality that represents the possible number of piano lessons x and saxophone lessons y you can take this summer.

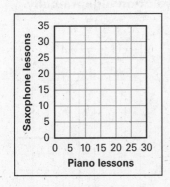

26. Is it possible to take 12 piano lessons and 15 saxophone lessons this summer?

27. If you take 14 piano lessons, what is the maximum number of saxophone lessons you can take?

Name _____   Date _____

Match the linear system with its graph. Then classify the system as
consistent and independent, consistent and dependent, **or** *inconsistent.*

1. $3x - 2y = 2$
$-2x + y = -2$

2. $4x - y = 3$
$-8x + 2y = -6$

3. $x + 3y = 2$
$-3x - 9y = 18$

A.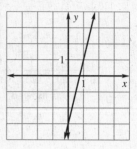

B.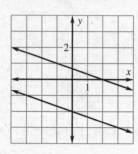

C.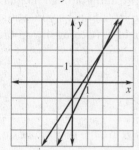

Graph the linear system and estimate the solution. Then check the
solution algebraically.

4. $2x + 3y = 8$
$-x + y = -4$

5. $3x + 5y = -4$
$2x - y = -7$

6. $x - 2y = 4$
$4x + 2y = 6$

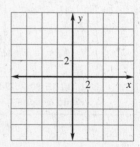

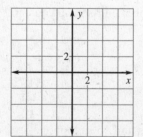

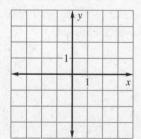

LESSON 3.1 **Practice** *continued*
For use with pages 152–159

7. $3x + y = 3$
$-2x + y = 3$

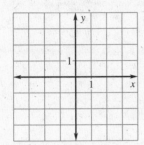

8. $5x - 2y = -1$
$x - 3y = 5$

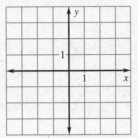

9. $x - 2y = -5$
$-2x + 6y = 18$

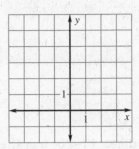

10. $3x + 3y = 3$
$x + 2y = 0$

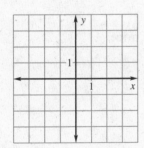

11. $2x - 4y = 2$
$-2x + 3y = 0$

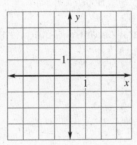

12. $5x - 3y = -17$
$4x + 5y = 16$

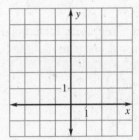

Solve the system. Then classify the system as *consistent and independent*, *consistent and dependent*, or *inconsistent*.

13. $x - 2y = 5$
$2x - 4y = 10$

14. $5x + y = 16$
$-3x + y = 0$

15. $2x + \frac{1}{2}y = 4$
$12x - 6y = -12$

LESSON 3.1 Practice *continued*
For use with pages 152–159

16. **Concert** A vendor sold 200 tickets for an upcoming rock concert. Floor seats were $36 and stadium seats were $28. The vendor sold $6080 in tickets. How many $36 and $28 tickets did the vendor sell?

In Exercises 17–20, use the following information.

Break-Even Analysis You purchase a music store for $115,000. The estimated monthly revenue is $5500 and expected monthly costs are $3200.

17. Let R represent the revenue during the first t months. Write a linear model for R.

18. Let C represent the costs during the first t months including the purchase price. Write a linear model for C.

19. Graph the revenue and cost linear models on the same coordinate plane.

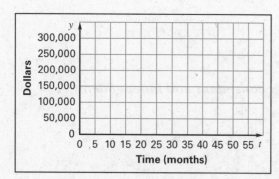

20. How many months will it take until revenue and costs are equal (the "break-even point")?

LESSON 3.2 Practice

For use with pages 160–167

Solve the system using the substitution method.

1. $x + 2y = 6$
$3x - 2y = 2$

2. $x + 3y = 3$
$2x - 4y = 6$

3. $4x + y = 7$
$2x + 5y = -1$

4. $2x - 3y = 3$
$-2x + y = -4$

5. $3x + 2y = -2$
$6x - y = 6$

6. $8x + 2y = 2$
$x + 3y = 14$

Solve the system using the elimination method.

7. $-3x + 3y = 3$
$3x + y = 9$

8. $5x - y = -9$
$2x + y = 2$

9. $-5x + 12y = 20$
$x - 2y = -6$

10. $4x - 2y = -2$
$6x + y = 5$

11. $3x + 2y = 1$
$4x + 6y = 7$

12. $7x - 3y = 6$
$-2x + 5y = -10$

Solve the system using any algebraic method.

13. $5x + 7y = -2$
$2x - 7y = 9$

14. $x + 3y = 1$
$3x + 7y = 1$

15. $4x + 6y = 8$
$2x + 3y = 3$

Practice *continued*

For use with pages 160–167

16. $8x - 5y = -17$
$-2x + y = 6$

17. $3x - 8y = 0$
$-2x + 5y = -2$

18. $4x - 6y = 2$
$5x + 3y = 1$

19. $2x - 5y = 3$
$-4x + 10y = -6$

20. $8x + 3y = 10$
$-6x + y = -12$

21. $5x + 4y = -18$
$2x + 3y = -24$

22. CDs and Cassettes From 1990 to 1998, the manufacturer's shipments for audio cassettes A (in millions) and compact discs C (in millions) can be modeled by the equations

$A = -31.8t + 322$ Audio cassette shipments

$C = 42.8t + 110$ Compact disc shipments

where t is the number of years since 1990. During what year did the number of compact discs shipped surpass the number of audio cassettes shipped?

23. Hair Salon A hair salon receives a shipment of 84 bottles of hair conditioner to use and sell to customers. The two types of conditioners received are type A, which is used for regular hair, and type B, which is used for dry hair. Type A costs $6.50 per bottle and type B costs $8.25 per bottle. The hair salon's invoice for the conditioner is $588. How many of each type of conditioner are in the shipment?

24. Birthday Gift You and your sister decide to combine your weekly overtime earnings to buy a birthday gift for your mother. Your overtime rate is $18 per hour and your sister's overtime rate is $24 per hour. The total amount earned for the gift was $288. If you worked two more hours of overtime than your sister, how many overtime hours did each of you work?

Name _____ Date _____

13. $8x - 2y + z = -6$
$-x + 3y - 2z = -15$
$3x - y + 4z = 13$

14. $2x + 2y + z = -5$
$2x + y + 3z = 7$
$-4x - 2y - 6z = -14$

15. $3x - 4y - 4z = 8$
$4x + 2y - 2z = 11$
$-5x + 8y + 3z = -9$

16. Harvest Yields A farmer makes three deliveries to the feed mill during one harvest. The harvest produced 2885 bushels of corn, 1335 bushels of wheat, and 1230 bushels of soybeans. Use the table to write and solve a system of equations to find the total number of bushels in each delivery.

Crop	1st Delivery	2nd Delivery	3rd Delivery
Corn	50%	75%	40%
Wheat	30%	10%	30%
Soybeans	20%	15%	30%

17. Harvest Earnings The feed mill pays a farmer $6930.00 for the 1st delivery, $5475.00 for the 2nd delivery, and $8879.50 for the 3rd delivery. The table shows the number of bushels included in each delivery. Use the table to write and solve a system of equations to find the price per bushel that the farmer received for each crop.

Delivery	Corn	Wheat	Soybeans
1st Delivery	900	540	360
2nd Delivery	1125	150	225
3rd Delivery	860	645	645

LESSON 3.5 Practice
For use with pages 187–194

Perform the indicated operation, if possible. If not possible, state the reason.

1. $\begin{bmatrix} 2 & 1 \\ 6 & 4 \end{bmatrix} - \begin{bmatrix} -2 & 1 \\ -4 & 0 \end{bmatrix}$

2. $\begin{bmatrix} 5 & 2 \\ -1 & 4 \\ -3 & 6 \end{bmatrix} + \begin{bmatrix} -2 & 4 \\ 6 & -2 \\ 7 & -5 \end{bmatrix}$

3. $\begin{bmatrix} 6 & 4 & 3 \\ 1 & -3 & 2 \\ 8 & 7 & 1 \end{bmatrix} - \begin{bmatrix} 4 & 5 & -4 \\ 5 & 1 & 0 \\ 6 & 4 & 7 \end{bmatrix}$

4. $\begin{bmatrix} -4 & 2 & 3 \end{bmatrix} + \begin{bmatrix} -2 \\ 0 \\ -1 \end{bmatrix}$

5. $\begin{bmatrix} 10 & -5 & 7 \\ 2 & -12 & 0 \\ 8 & -4 & 6 \end{bmatrix} + \begin{bmatrix} -7 & 14 & 6 \\ 0 & 12 & -4 \\ 2 & 7 & 3 \end{bmatrix}$

6. $\begin{bmatrix} 10 & -7 & 14 \\ -5 & -10 & 0 \\ 9 & -3 & -7 \end{bmatrix} - \begin{bmatrix} -1 & -3 & 8 \\ -12 & 0 & 6 \\ 10 & -5 & 5 \end{bmatrix}$

Perform the indicated operation.

7. $-3 \begin{bmatrix} 4 & 2 \\ 3 & 2 \end{bmatrix}$

8. $-2 \begin{bmatrix} 3 & 0 & -1 \\ 0.5 & -6 & 4 \\ 7 & -1.25 & 9 \end{bmatrix}$

9. $-4 \begin{bmatrix} 4 & 1 \\ -5 & 0 \\ 1. & -3 \end{bmatrix}$

Practice *continued*
For use with pages 187–194

Solve the matrix equation for x and y.

10. $\begin{bmatrix} -2x & 6 \\ 3y & 9 \end{bmatrix} = \begin{bmatrix} -8 & 6 \\ -12 & 9 \end{bmatrix}$

11. $\begin{bmatrix} 4 & 5x \\ -2 & 5 \end{bmatrix} + \begin{bmatrix} -11 & 2 \\ 6 & 5 \end{bmatrix} = \begin{bmatrix} y & 12 \\ 4 & 10 \end{bmatrix}$

In Exercises 12–15, use the following information.

Book Prices The matrices below show the number of books sold and the average price (in dollars) for the years 2002, 2003, and 2004.

	2002 (A)		2003 (B)		2004 (C)	
	Sold	Price	Sold	Price	Sold	Price
Book A	125,000	52.00	110,000	55.50	90,000	47.50
Book B	85,000	83.50	95,000	85.50	100,000	89.00
Book C	190,000	45.60	210,000	56.25	225,000	75.25

12. You purchased book A in 2002, book C in 2003, and book B in 2004. How much did you spend on these three books?

13. How many more (or less) volumes of book B were sold in 2004 than in 2002?

14. How much more (or less) is the price of book A in 2004 than in 2002?

15. In 2005, would you expect book C sales to be *more* or *less* than 100,000?

Name _____ Date _____

State the dimensions of each matrix and determine whether the product AB is defined. If so, give the dimensions of AB.

1. $A = \begin{bmatrix} 2 & 1 \\ 5 & 0 \\ 1 & 2 \end{bmatrix}, B = \begin{bmatrix} 2 & 1 & 5 \end{bmatrix}$

2. $A = \begin{bmatrix} 2 & -3 & 4 \\ -2 & 1 & 0 \end{bmatrix}, B = \begin{bmatrix} 1 & 2 & 0 \\ 5 & 4 & 3 \\ -4 & 2 & -5 \end{bmatrix}$

Find the product. If it is not defined, state the reason.

3. $\begin{bmatrix} 3 & 2 \end{bmatrix} \begin{bmatrix} 1 \\ 4 \end{bmatrix}$

4. $\begin{bmatrix} 1 & -1 \\ 2 & 1 \end{bmatrix} \begin{bmatrix} 2 & -2 \\ 1 & 2 \end{bmatrix}$

5. $\begin{bmatrix} 2 \\ -1 \\ 3 \end{bmatrix} \begin{bmatrix} -1 & 3 \end{bmatrix}$

6. $\begin{bmatrix} 3 & 5 \\ -2 & 4 \end{bmatrix} \begin{bmatrix} 2 & -1 \\ 4 & 0 \end{bmatrix}$

7. $\begin{bmatrix} 5 & 1 & 0 \\ -2 & 3 & 1 \\ 0 & 2 & 4 \end{bmatrix} \begin{bmatrix} -1 & 2 & -3 \\ 0 & 5 & 4 \\ 2 & -1 & 2 \end{bmatrix}$

8. $\begin{bmatrix} 2 \\ 1 \end{bmatrix} \begin{bmatrix} 1 & 2 & 4 \\ -2 & 3 & 1 \end{bmatrix}$

9. $\begin{bmatrix} -1 & 6 & 2 & 4 \end{bmatrix} \begin{bmatrix} 1 \\ -1 \\ 4 \\ 0 \end{bmatrix}$

LESSON
3.6

Practice *continued*
For use with pages 195–202

10. $\begin{bmatrix} 2 & -3 \\ 4 & -2 \\ 0 & -1 \end{bmatrix} \begin{bmatrix} 2 & 1 & -1 \\ 5 & 3 & 2 \end{bmatrix}$

11. $\begin{bmatrix} 0 & 1 & 0 \\ 2 & 3 & -1 \\ -2 & 4 & 0 \\ 5 & 0 & -2 \end{bmatrix} \begin{bmatrix} 2 \\ -3 \\ 1 \end{bmatrix}$

Using the given matrices, evaluate the expression.

$A = \begin{bmatrix} 2 & -1 \\ 3 & 2 \end{bmatrix}, B = \begin{bmatrix} 1 & 0 \\ 3 & -2 \end{bmatrix}, C = \begin{bmatrix} 3 & -2 \\ -1 & 4 \end{bmatrix}$

12. $-2BC$

13. $AC - AB$

14. $BA + BC$

15. **Football** Tickets to the football game cost $2.50 for students, $5.00 for adults, and $4.00 for senior citizens. Attendance for the first game of the postseason was 120 students, 185 adults, and 34 senior citizens. Attendance for the second game of the postseason was 150 students, 210 adults, and 50 senior citizens. Use matrix multiplication to find the revenue from ticket sales for each game.

LESSON 3.7 **Practice**
For use with pages 203–209

Evaluate the determinant of the matrix.

1. $\begin{bmatrix} 5 & -2 \\ 4 & -4 \end{bmatrix}$

2. $\begin{bmatrix} 3 & -5 \\ -2 & -3 \end{bmatrix}$

3. $\begin{bmatrix} \frac{1}{2} & \frac{2}{3} \\ 6 & 5 \end{bmatrix}$

Evaluate the determinant of the matrix.

4. $\begin{bmatrix} 5 & -1 & 3 \\ 4 & 0 & 2 \\ 1 & -2 & -5 \end{bmatrix}$

5. $\begin{bmatrix} 3 & 2 & 9 \\ 0 & 1 & -4 \\ 5 & -1 & 2 \end{bmatrix}$

6. $\begin{bmatrix} 1 & 15 & 2 \\ 0 & 1 & 3 \\ 2 & 12 & 2 \end{bmatrix}$

7. $\begin{bmatrix} 12 & -8 & 3 \\ -1 & 2 & 0 \\ -15 & 1 & 3 \end{bmatrix}$

8. $\begin{bmatrix} 7 & 5 & 6 \\ 3 & 4 & 5 \\ 6 & 1 & 4 \end{bmatrix}$

9. $\begin{bmatrix} 3 & 0 & -2 \\ 0 & 7 & 0 \\ -5 & -4 & 6 \end{bmatrix}$

Find the area of the triangle with the given vertices.

10.
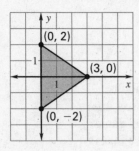

11.
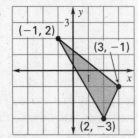

12.
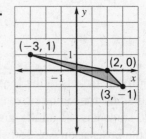

Algebra 2
Chapter 3 Practice Workbook

LESSON 3.7 **Practice** *continued*
For use with pages 203–209

Use Cramer's rule to solve the linear system.

13. $x - 5y = -1$
$-2x + 5y = -3$

14. $x + 2y = 1$
$-3x - 7y = -6$

15. $2x + 6y = 12$
$-x + 7y = -6$

16. $2x + 2y + z = 2$
$-x + 3y + z = -2$
$3x + 2z = 7$

17. $2x - 5y + 2z = 2$
$-3x + y - 6z = 3$
$x + y + z = 1$

18. $3x + 2y + 3z = -1$
$2x - 8y + 2z = -3$
$x + 6y + 4z = -2$

In Exercises 19 and 20, use the following information.

Gasoline You fill up your car with 15 gallons of premium gasoline and fill up a 5 gallon gas can with regular gasoline for various appliances around the house. You pay the cashier $42. The price of regular gasoline y is 20 cents less per gallon than the price of premium gasoline x.

19. Write a system of linear equations that models the price per gallon for regular and premium gasoline.

20. Use Cramer's rule to find the price per gallon of regular and premium gasoline.

Name _____   Date _____

 Practice
For use with pages 210–217

Find the inverse of the matrix, if it exists.

1. $\begin{bmatrix} 4 & 7 \\ 1 & 2 \end{bmatrix}$

2. $\begin{bmatrix} 3 & 2 \\ 4 & 2 \end{bmatrix}$

3. $\begin{bmatrix} 4 & -2 \\ 3 & 1 \end{bmatrix}$

4. $\begin{bmatrix} 7 & 14 \\ 3 & 6 \end{bmatrix}$

5. $\begin{bmatrix} -4 & -2 \\ 5 & 2 \end{bmatrix}$

6. $\begin{bmatrix} 3 & -3 \\ -3 & -2 \end{bmatrix}$

Use a graphing calculator to find the inverse of the matrix.

7. $\begin{bmatrix} 1 & 3 & 5 \\ 0 & 3 & 5 \\ 0 & 0 & 5 \end{bmatrix}$

8. $\begin{bmatrix} 0 & 1 & 0 \\ 2 & 1 & -2 \\ 0 & 2 & 2 \end{bmatrix}$

Solve the matrix equation.

9. $\begin{bmatrix} 2 & 1 \\ 3 & 2 \end{bmatrix} X = \begin{bmatrix} 5 & 1 \\ 2 & 1 \end{bmatrix}$

10. $\begin{bmatrix} 4 & 3 \\ 2 & 2 \end{bmatrix} X = \begin{bmatrix} -2 & 3 \\ -1 & 2 \end{bmatrix}$

11. $\begin{bmatrix} 3 & 1 \\ 6 & 3 \end{bmatrix} X = \begin{bmatrix} 1 & 4 & -2 \\ 6 & 0 & -3 \end{bmatrix}$

12. $\begin{bmatrix} 6 & 2 \\ 5 & 1 \end{bmatrix} X = \begin{bmatrix} 9 & 12 & 6 \\ -4 & 3 & 8 \end{bmatrix}$

LESSON 3.8 **Practice** *continued*
For use with pages 210–217

Use an inverse matrix to solve the linear system.

13. $3x - 2y = 2$
$2x - y = 2$

14. $5x + 3y = 4$
$2x + 2y = 8$

15. $-x + 6y = 20$
$x - 9y = -12$

16. $2x + z = 2$
$5x - y + z = 5$
$-x + 2y + 2z = 0$

17. $3x + y + 2z = 9$
$-2x + 2y + 3z = 6$
$2x - y + z = 8$

18. $3x + 3y + 3z = -12$
$5x + 2y + 2z = -17$
$2x - 4y - z = -20$

In Exercises 19–21, use the following information.

NBA During the 2004–2005 NBA season, Shaquille O'Neal scored 1669 points while making 1011 shots. Shaq's points were a combination of 3-point field goals, 2-point field goals, and 1-point free throws. He made 305 more 2-point field goals than free throws.

19. Write a system of equations for the number of shots made during the season.

20. Write the system of equations from Exercise 19 as a matrix equation $AX = B$.

21. Use an inverse matrix to solve the system of equations. How many of each type of shot did Shaq make during the season?

Algebra 2

Name _____ Date _____

For the following functions (a) tell whether the graph *opens up* or *opens down*, (b) find the vertex, and (c) find the axis of symmetry.

1. $y = -3x^2 + 1$

2. $y = -2x^2 - 1$

3. $y = 3x^2 - 2x$

4. $y = -4x^2 - 2x + 9$

5. $y = 5x^2 - 5x + 7$

6. $y = -2x^2 - 3x + 3$

Match the equation with its graph.

7. $y = -x^2 + 5x - 2$

8. $y = -x^2 - 5x - 2$

9. $y = -\frac{1}{4}x^2 + 2$

A.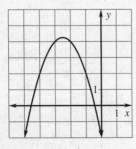

B.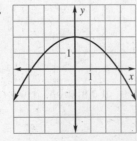

C.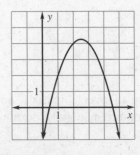

LESSON 4.1 **Practice** _continued_
For use with pages 236–244

Graph the function. Label the vertex and axis of symmetry.

10. $y = x^2 - 3$

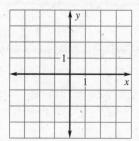

11. $y = -2x^2 + 4x$

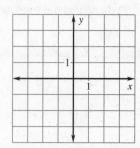

12. $y = 2x^2 + 6x + 1$

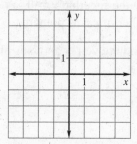

13. $y = 4x^2 - 16x + 3$

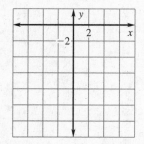

14. $y = -3x^2 - 12x + 1$

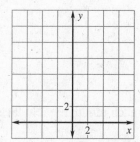

15. $y = \frac{1}{3}x^2 + 2x - 1$

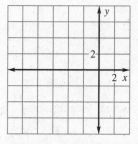

16. $y = x^2 + 5x - 1$

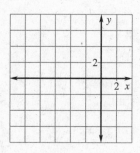

17. $y = 3x^2 + 3x - 2$

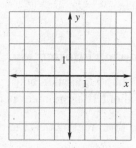

18. $y = -5x^2 + 4x + 2$

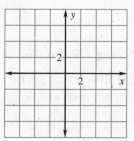

19. $y = -\frac{1}{2}x^2 + 3x - 1$

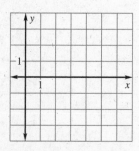

20. $y = -2x^2 - 4x + 3$

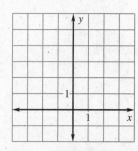

21. $y = 2x^2 - 4x - 2$

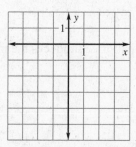

Practice *continued*
For use with pages 236–244

In Exercises 22–24, use the following information.

Minimize Cost A baker has modeled the monthly operating costs for making wedding cakes by the function $y = 0.5x^2 - 12x + 150$ where y is the total cost in dollars and x is the number of cakes prepared.

22. Find the vertex and axis of symmetry.

23. What is the minimum cost?

24. How many cakes should be prepared each month to yield the minimum cost?

In Exercises 25 and 26, use the following information.

Maximize Revenue A sports store sells about 50 mountain bikes per month at a price of $220 each. For each $20 decrease in price, about 10 more bikes per month are sold.

25. Write a quadratic function in standard form that models the revenue from bike sales.

26. What price produces the maximum revenue?

Name _____   Date _____

LESSON
4.2

Practice

For use with pages 245–251

Match the equation with its graph.

1. $y = 2(x - 2)^2 + 1$

2. $y = -(x - 3)(x - 1)$

3. $y = -(x + 1)^2 + 2$

A.
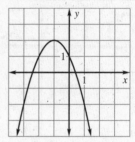

B.
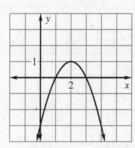

C.
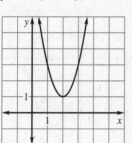

Graph the function. Label the vertex and axis of symmetry.

4. $y = (x + 1)^2 + 3$

5. $y = (x - 2)^2 - 1$

6. $y = (x + 2)^2 - 3$

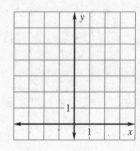

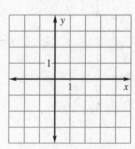

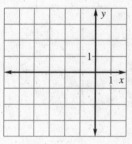

7. $y = -2(x + 1)^2 - 4$

8. $y = 2(x + 2)^2 - 4$

9. $y = -(x - 4)^2 + 8$

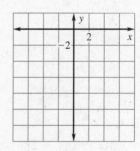

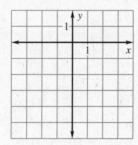

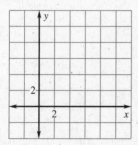

Name _____ Date _____

Practice *continued*
For use with pages 245–251

Graph the function. Label the vertex, axis of symmetry, and *x*-intercepts.

10. $y = (x + 2)(x - 4)$ **11.** $y = (x + 2)(x + 3)$ **12.** $y = (x + 4)(x + 2)$

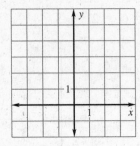 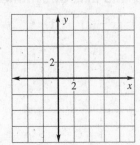 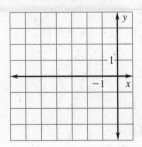

13. $y = -(x - 3)(x + 1)$ **14.** $y = 3(x - 1)(x - 4)$ **15.** $y = -3x(x + 7)$

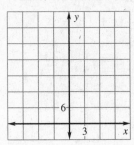

Write the quadratic function in standard form.

16. $y = (x - 2)^2 + 6$ **17.** $y = -2(x + 1)^2 + 3$ **18.** $y = 3(x - 3)^2 - 12$

19. $y = (x - 4)(x - 2)$ **20.** $y = 4(x + 1)(x + 2)$ **21.** $y = -3(x - 3)(x + 2)$

LESSON
4.2

Practice *continued*
For use with pages 245–251

Find the minimum value or the maximum value of the function.

22. $y = (x - 6)^2 + 3$ **23.** $y = -(x - 3)^2 - 4$ **24.** $y = 3(x - 3)^2 - 3$

25. $y = (x + 7)(x + 3)$ **26.** $y = 2(x - 3)(x - 5)$ **27.** $y = -(x - 1)(x + 4)$

28. Visual Thinking Use a graphing calculator to graph $y = a(x - 2)(x - 6)$ where $a = \frac{1}{2}$, 1, and 4. Use the same viewing window for all three graphs. How do the graphs change as a increases?

In Exercises 29 and 30, use the following information.

Golf The flight of a particular golf shot can be modeled by the function $y = -0.001x(x - 260)$ where x is the horizontal distance (in yards) from the impact point and y is the height (in yards). The graph is shown below.

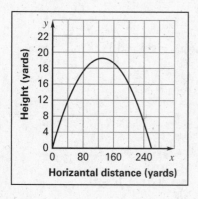

29. How many yards away from the impact point does the golf ball land?

30. What is the maximum height in yards of the golf shot?

LESSON 4.3 **Practice**
For use with pages 252–258

Factor the expression. If the expression cannot be factored, say so.

1. $x^2 + 4x - 21$

2. $x^2 - 6x + 5$

3. $x^2 + 6x + 8$

4. $x^2 - x - 6$

5. $x^2 - x - 12$

6. $x^2 - 2x - 8$

7. $x^2 - 9x + 20$

8. $x^2 + 3x - 18$

9. $x^2 - 9$

10. $x^2 + 8x + 16$

11. $x^2 - 11x + 28$

12. $x^2 - 2x + 2$

13. $x^2 + 4x - 32$

14. $x^2 - 3x - 10$

15. $x^2 - 25$

16. $x^2 - 9x + 14$

17. $x^2 - 100$

18. $x^2 - 8x - 15$

Solve the equation.

19. $x^2 + x - 6 = 0$

20. $x^2 + 3x - 10 = 0$

21. $x^2 - 5x + 6 = 0$

22. $x^2 - 4x + 4 = 0$

23. $x^2 + 7x + 12 = 0$

24. $x^2 - 3x - 28 = 0$

Algebra 2

**LESSON
4.3** **Practice** *continued*
For use with pages 252–258

25. $x^2 - 36 = 0$ **26.** $x^2 - 2x - 15 = 0$ **27.** $x^2 - 11x + 18 = 0$

28. $3x^2 = 48$ **29.** $x^2 - 7x - 4 = -10$ **30.** $9x - 8 = x^2$

Find the zeros of the function by rewriting the function in intercept form.

31. $y = x^2 + 8x + 15$ **32.** $y = x^2 - 12x + 32$ **33.** $f(x) = x^2 - 2x - 35$

34. $y = x^2 - x - 30$ **35.** $g(x) = x^2 + 10x + 9$ **36.** $y = x^2 - 6x$

37. $h(x) = x^2 - 12x + 27$ **38.** $y = x^2 - 9$ **39.** $y = x^2 + 16x + 64$

40. **Picture Frame** You are making a square frame of uniform width for a square picture that has side lengths of 2 feet. The total area of the frame is 5 square feet. What is the length of the sides of the frame?

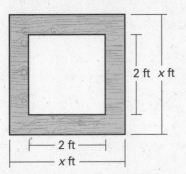

41. **Concert Stage** The dimensions of the old stage at the concert hall were 30 feet wide and 15 feet deep. The new stage has a total area of 1000 square feet. The dimensions of the new stage were created by adding the same distance x to the width and the depth of the old stage dimensions. What is the value of x?

LESSON
4.4 **Practice**
For use with pages 259–265

Factor the expression. If the expression cannot be factored, say so.

1. $3x^2 + 10x - 8$ **2.** $2x^2 + 5x - 3$ **3.** $4x^2 + 4x + 1$

4. $2x^2 - 5x + 1$ **5.** $4x^2 + 5x - 6$ **6.** $2x^2 + 11x + 15$

7. $9x^2 + 12x + 4$ **8.** $12x^2 - 24x - 9$ **9.** $18x^2 - 2$

10. $12x^2 + 17x + 6$ **11.** $15x^2 + 8x - 16$ **12.** $4x^2 - 5$

13. $12x^2 - 39x + 9$ **14.** $18x^2 - 9x - 14$ **15.** $20x^2 - 54x + 36$

16. $42x^2 + 35x + 7$ **17.** $-12x^2 - x + 11$ **18.** $80x^2 + 68x + 12$

Solve the equation.

19. $2x^2 + 3x - 2 = 0$ **20.** $2x^2 - 3x - 9 = 0$

21. $4x^2 - 8x + 3 = 0$ **22.** $9x^2 - 4 = 0$

LESSON 4.4 **Practice** *continued*
For use with pages 259–265

23. $8x^2 - 6x + 1 = 0$

24. $18x^2 + 48x = -32$

25. $9x^2 + 11x + 18 = -10x + 8$

26. $5x^2 - 2x - 6 = -3x^2 + 6x$

27. $5x^2 - 3x + 3 = -2x^2 + 3$

28. $25x^2 - 24x - 9 = -7x^2 + 12x - 18$

Find the zeros of the function by rewriting the function in intercept form.

29. $y = 3x^2 + 2x$

30. $y = 12x^2 + 8x - 15$

31. $f(x) = 5x^2 - 25x + 30$

32. $y = 25x^2 + 10x - 24$

33. $g(x) = 33x^2 - 9x - 24$

34. $y = 4x^2 + 1$

Find the value of x.

35. Area of the triangle = 27

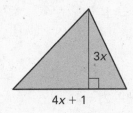

$3x$

$4x + 1$

36. Area of the rectangle = 22

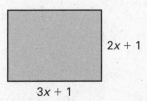

$2x + 1$

$3x + 1$

37. **Picture Frame** You are making a frame of uniform width for a picture that is to be displayed at the local museum. The picture is 3.25 feet tall and 3 feet wide. The museum has allocated 15 square feet of wall space to display the picture. What should the width of the frame be in order to use all of the allocated space?

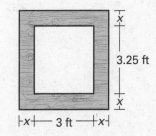

x

3.25 ft

x

x — 3 ft — x

Name _____ Date _____

Practice
For use with pages 266–271

Simplify the expression.

1. $\sqrt{242}$

2. $\sqrt{153}$

3. $\sqrt{56}$

4. $5\sqrt{24} \cdot 2\sqrt{28}$

5. $\sqrt{8} \cdot 3\sqrt{40} \cdot \sqrt{3}$

6. $\sqrt{10} \cdot \sqrt{14}$

7. $\sqrt{\dfrac{121}{225}}$

8. $\sqrt{\dfrac{7}{9}} \cdot \sqrt{\dfrac{4}{7}}$

9. $\sqrt{24} \cdot \sqrt{\dfrac{80}{192}}$

10. $\dfrac{3}{4 + \sqrt{5}}$

11. $\dfrac{-6}{5 - \sqrt{11}}$

12. $\dfrac{7 - \sqrt{7}}{10 + \sqrt{3}}$

Solve the equation.

13. $x^2 = 289$

14. $x^2 - 169 = 0$

15. $2x^2 - 512 = 0$

16. $3x^2 - 150 = 282$

17. $\dfrac{1}{2}x^2 - 8 = 16$

18. $\dfrac{2}{3}x^2 - 4 = 12$

19. $2x^2 + 5 = 5x^2 - 37$

20. $4(x^2 - 8) = 84$

21. $3(x^2 + 2) = 18$

22. $2(x + 2)^2 = 72$

23. $3(x - 3)^2 + 2 = 26$

24. $(3x + 2)^2 - 49 = 0$

25. $(4x - 5)^2 = 64$

26. $\dfrac{1}{2}(x - 4)^2 = 8$

27. $\dfrac{2}{3}(x + 8)^2 - 66 = 0$

Name _____ Date _____

Practice *continued*

For use with pages 266–271

When an object is dropped, its height *h* can be determined after
t seconds by using the falling object model $h = -16t^2 + s$ where *s* is
the initial height. Find the time it takes an object to hit the ground
when it is dropped from a height of *s* feet.

28. $s = 160$

29. $s = 300$

30. $s = 550$

31. $s = 690$

32. $s = 900$

33. $s = 1600$

Use the Pythagorean theorem to find *x*. Round to the nearest hundredth.

34.

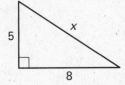

35.

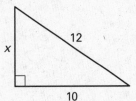

36. Operating Costs For a period of 48 months, the average monthly operating cost for
a small business *C* (in dollars) can be approximated by the model $C = 0.55t^2 + 550$
where *t* is the number of months. During which month was the average operating
cost $1430?

LESSON 4.6 **Practice**
For use with pages 275–282

Solve the equation.

1. $x^2 = -36$

2. $x^2 + 121 = 0$

3. $x^2 + 9 = 4$

4. $x^2 = 2x^2 + 4$

5. $3x^2 + 40 = -x^2 - 56$

6. $11x^2 = -5x^2 - 1$

7. $(x - 3)^2 = -12$

8. $-2(x - 1)^2 = 36$

9. $4(x + 2)^2 + 320 = 0$

Write the expression as a complex number in standard form.

10. $(1 + i) + (3 + i)$

11. $(4 - 3i) + (2 + 6i)$

12. $(-4 - i) - (4 + 5i)$

13. $(5 - 3i) + (-3 - 6i)$

14. $3i(4 + 2i)$

15. $-2i(3 - i)$

16. $(2 + i)(4 + 2i)$

17. $(5 - 2i)(1 - 3i)$

18. $-(3 + i)(7 - 3i)$

19. $-2i(1 + i)(2 + 3i)$

20. $(2 - i)^2$

21. $(5 + 3i)(5 - 3i)$

22. $\dfrac{5}{3 - 2i}$

23. $\dfrac{2 - i}{3 + 4i}$

24. $\dfrac{1 + 2i}{\sqrt{2} + i}$

25. $\dfrac{3}{2 - 4i} - (3 + 2i)$

Algebra 2
Chapter 4 Practice Workbook

LESSON 4.6 **Practice** *continued*
For use with pages 275–282

Find the absolute value of the complex number.

26. $3 - 4i$ **27.** $1 - i\sqrt{3}$ **28.** $\sqrt{5} + 2i\sqrt{2}$

Plot the numbers in a complex plane.

29. $3i$ **30.** $2 + 2i$ **31.** $-2 - 3i$

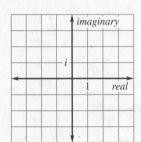 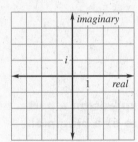 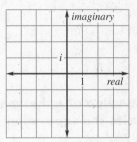

Using the properties of exponents, write the complex number in standard form.

32. $2 + i^2$ **33.** $3 + i^3$ **34.** $5 - i^4$ **35.** $2 - i^5$

36. $1 + i^4$ **37.** $1 + i^8$ **38.** $1 + i^{12}$ **39.** $1 + i^{16}$

40. **Pattern Recognition** Using the information from Exercises 36–39, write a general statement about the value of i^n where n is a positive factor of 4. Use this statement to write $2 + i^{207}$ in standard form.

LESSON 4.7 **Practice**
For use with pages 283–291

Solve the equation by finding square roots.

1. $x^2 + 8x + 16 = 9$ **2.** $x^2 - 6x + 9 = 25$ **3.** $x^2 - 12x + 36 = 49$

4. $2x^2 - 12x + 18 = 32$ **5.** $4x^2 - 4x + 1 = 36$ **6.** $5x^2 - 20x + 20 = 35$

7. $x^2 - \frac{2}{3}x + \frac{1}{9} = 1$ **8.** $x^2 + \frac{3}{2}x + \frac{9}{16} = 3$ **9.** $9x^2 + 12x + 4 = 5$

Find the value of c that makes the expression a perfect square trinomial. Then write the expression as a square of a binomial.

10. $x^2 + 8x + c$ **11.** $x^2 - 22x + c$

12. $x^2 + 16x + c$ **13.** $x^2 + 3x + c$

14. $x^2 - 9x + c$ **15.** $9x^2 - 12x + c$

Solve the equation by completing the square.

16. $x^2 + 4x = 1$ **17.** $x^2 - 10x = -10$

18. $x^2 - 2x - 9 = 0$ **19.** $x^2 + 6x + 10 = 0$

20. $x^2 + 8x + 4 = 0$ **21.** $3x^2 + 36x = -42$

Algebra 2
Chapter 4 Practice Workbook

Practice *continued*
For use with pages 283–291

22. $x^2 - 24x + 81 = 0$

23. $4x^2 + 20x + 25 = 0$

24. $3x^2 - 3x + 9 = 0$

25. $6x^2 - 12x - 18 = 0$

Write the quadratic function in vertex form. Then identify the vertex.

26. $y = x^2 + 14x + 11$

27. $y = x^2 - 8x + 10$

28. $y = 2x^2 + 4x - 5$

29. $y = 3x^2 - 9x + 18$

Find the value of *x*.

30. Area of rectangle = 84

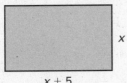

x

$x + 5$

31. Area of triangle = 20

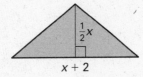

$\frac{1}{2}x$

$x + 2$

32. **Shot Put** In a track and field event, a contestant had a throw in the shot put that can be modeled by $y = -0.02x^2 + x + 6$ where x is the shot put's horizontal distance (in feet) and y is the corresponding height (in feet). How long was the throw? Round the answer to the nearest tenth.

LESSON 4.8 **Practice**
For use with pages 292–299

Find the discriminant of the quadratic equation.

1. $x^2 - 3x + 5 = 0$

2. $2x^2 + x + 2 = 0$

3. $4x^2 - 9x + 2 = 0$

4. $-3x^2 + 6x - 3 = 0$

5. $3x^2 + 3x - 1 = 0$

6. $7x^2 - 4x + 5 = 0$

Find the discriminant and use it to determine if the solution has *one real*, *two real*, or *two imaginary* solution(s).

7. $x^2 + 4x + 3 = 0$

8. $x^2 - 2x + 4 = 0$

9. $x^2 - 2x + 1 = 0$

10. $3x^2 + 2x - 1 = 0$

11. $-x^2 - x = 4$

12. $5x^2 - 4x + 1 = 3x + 4$

Use the quadratic formula to solve the equation.

13. $x^2 + 4x - 2 = 0$

14. $2x^2 - 5x - 2 = 0$

15. $x^2 + 2x = 4x$

16. $-6x^2 + 3x + 2 = 3$

17. $-x^2 + 1 = -5x^2 + 4x$

18. $2(x - 3)^2 = -2x + 9$

19. $2.5x^2 - 2.8x = 0.4$

20. $4.8x^2 = 5.2x + 2.7$

LESSON 4.8 **Practice** *continued*
For use with pages 292–299

Solve the equation using the quadratic formula. Then solve the equation by factoring to check your solution(s).

21. $x^2 - 2x - 24 = 0$

22. $x^2 - 2x + 1 = 0$

23. $2x^2 - 9x + 9 = 0$

24. $6x^2 + 17x + 5 = 0$

25. $10x^2 + x = 2$

26. $6x^2 = 5x + 6$

27. New Carpet You have new carpeting installed in a rectangular room. You are charged for 28 square yards of carpet and 60 feet (20 yards) of tack strip. Tack strip is used along the perimeter to secure the carpet in place. Do you think these figures are correct? *Explain* your answer.

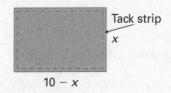

Tack strip

x

$10 - x$

In Exercises 28–31, use the following information.

Launched Object An object is launched upward with an initial velocity of 64 feet per second from a platform 80 feet high.

28. Write a height model for the object.

29. How many seconds until the maximum height is reached?

30. What will be the maximum height?

31. How many seconds until the object hits the ground?

LESSON 4.9 **Practice**
For use with pages 300–307

Determine whether the ordered pair is a solution of the inequality.

1. $y < x^2 + 2x + 2$, $(1, 6)$

2. $y > x^2 - 5x$, $(2, -3)$

3. $y \leq 2x^2 - 7x$, $(4, 4)$

4. $y \geq -2x^2 + 3x - 6$, $(-1, -12)$

Match the inequality with its graph.

5. $y \geq x^2 + 4x - 1$

6. $y < -2x^2 + 3x - 5$

7. $y \leq \frac{1}{2}x^2 - x - 1$

A.

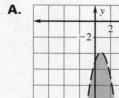

B.

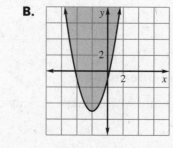

C.

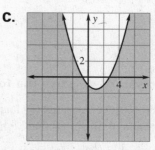

Graph the inequality.

8. $y \geq x^2 - 2$

9. $y < -x^2 - 2x + 1$

10. $y \leq x^2 - 3x + 15$

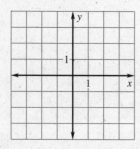

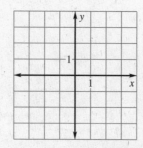

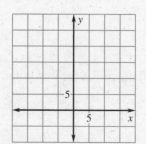

LESSON 4.9

Practice *continued*
For use with pages 300–307

11. $y > 3x^2 - 8x$

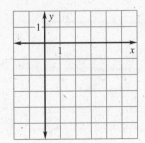

12. $y < -6x^2 + 2x + 3$

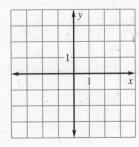

13. $y \geq 4x^2 - x - 7$

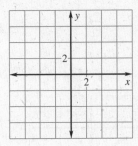

14. $y \geq x^2 + 2x - 8$

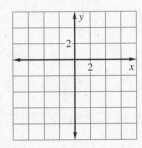

15. $y > -2x^2 - 14x + 21$

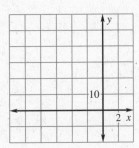

16. $y \leq 5x^2 + 2x - 6$

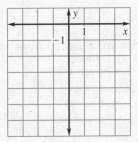

Match the system of inequalities with its graph.

17. $y > x^2 - 2x - 1$

$y < x^2 + 3x + 1$

A.

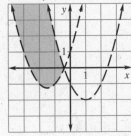

18. $y \leq -2x^2 - x + 2$

$y > \dfrac{2}{3}x^2 - 3$

B.

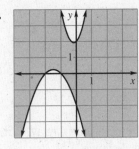

19. $y \leq 3x^2 + x + 2$

$y \geq -x^2 - 3x - 2$

C.

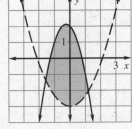

LESSON
4.9

Practice *continued*
For use with pages 300–307

Graph the system of inequalities.

20. $y \geq x^2 + 2x - 3$ **21.** $y \leq -\frac{1}{2}x^2 + 2x + 1$ **22.** $y < x^2 + 2x - 2$

$y < -x^2 - x - 2$ $y \leq -\frac{1}{2}x^2 - 2x + 1$ $y < x^2 - 2x - 2$

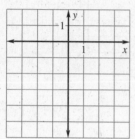   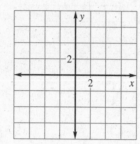   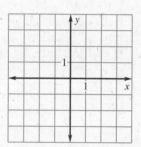

Solve the inequality algebraically.

23. $x^2 + x - 12 > 0$ **24.** $x^2 - 3x - 18 \leq 0$ **25.** $2x^2 + 13x + 6 < 0$

In Exercises 26–28, use the following information.

Football The path of a football kicked from the ground can be modeled by $h = -0.02x^2 + 1.2x$ where h is the height (in yards) and x is the horizontal distance (in yards) from where the ball is kicked. The crossbar on a field goal post is 10 feet above the ground.

26. Write an inequality to find the values of x where the ball is high enough to go over the crossbar.

27. Solve the inequality.

28. A player attempts to kick a field goal from 52 yards away. Will the ball have enough height to go over the crossbar from this distance?

Name _____ Date _____

Write a quadratic function in vertex form whose graph has the given vertex and passes through the given point.

1. vertex: $(0, 0)$

point: $(2, 4)$

2. vertex: $(2, 1)$

point: $(4, 5)$

3. vertex: $(2, -4)$

point: $(0, 0)$

4. vertex: $(-4, -2)$

point: $(-3, -1)$

5. vertex: $(3, -2)$

point: $(7, 6)$

6. vertex: $(4, -5)$

point: $(1, 13)$

Write a quadratic function in intercept form whose graph has the given *x*-intercepts and passes through the given point.

7. *x*-intercepts: 2, 3

point: $(4, 2)$

8. *x*-intercepts: -4, 1

point: $(-3, -4)$

9. *x*-intercepts: -5, 5

point: $(6, 11)$

10. *x*-intercepts: -7, -2

point: $(-5, -6)$

11. *x*-intercepts: 0, 4

point: $(-1, 20)$

12. *x*-intercepts: -3, -2

point: $(-4, -6)$

Name _____ Date _____

Write a quadratic function in standard form whose graph passes through the given points.

13. $(1, -2), (-2, 1), (3, 6)$

14. $(2, 6), (-2, -2), (1, 1)$

15. $(-2, 7), (-1, 3), (3, 7)$

16. $(1, 0), (2, 4), (0, 2)$

17. $(2, -4), (3, -7), (1, -3)$

18. $(-1, -2), (1, -4), (2, 1)$

In Exercises 19 and 20, use the following information.

Population Model The following table shows the population of a town from 1996 to 2004. Assume that t is the number of years since 1996 and P is measured in thousands of people.

Year, t	0	1	2	3	4	5	6	7	8
Population, P	22.8	25.0	26.5	27.1	27.8	28.1	27.9	26.9	26.1

19. Use a graphing calculator to find the best-fitting quadratic model for the data.

20. Using the model, what is the population in 2007?

In Exercises 21 and 22, use the following information.

Operating Costs The following table shows the operating costs of a small business from 2000 to 2005. Assume that t is the number of years since 2000 and C is the cost in thousands of dollars.

Year, t	0	1	2	3	4	5
Operating costs, C	2.3	2.6	3.1	3.3	4.0	5.2

21. Use a graphing calculator to find the best-fitting quadratic model for the data.

22. Using the model, how much are the operating costs in 2008?

Name _____   Date _____

Decide whether the function is a polynomial function. If it is, write the function in standard form and state the degree, type, and leading coefficient.

1. $f(x) = 7 - 2x$ **2.** $g(x) = 2x - x^3 + 8$ **3.** $h(x) = x^4 - x^{-3}$

Use direct substitution to evaluate the polynomial function for the given value of x.

4. $f(x) = 6x^4 - x^3 + 3x^2 - 5x + 9; x = -1$ **5.** $g(x) = 7x - x^4 + 1; x = -4$

Use synthetic substitution to evaluate the polynomial function for the given value of x.

6. $f(x) = 7x^4 - 3x^3 + x^2 + 5x - 9; x = 2$ **7.** $g(x) = x^3 - 8x + 6; x = -3$

Describe the end behavior of the graph of the polynomial function by completing these statements: $f(x) \to \underline{\ ?\ }$ **as** $x \to -\infty$ **and** $f(x) \to \underline{\ ?\ }$ **as** $x \to +\infty$.

8. $f(x) = -5x^3$ **9.** $f(x) = 2x^5 - 7x^2 - 4x$

10. $f(x) = 2x^8 + 9x^7 + 10$ **11.** $f(x) = -12x^6 - 2x + 5$

LESSON 5.2

Practice *continued*
For use with pages 336–345

Graph the polynomial function.

12. $f(x) = -x^3 - 2$

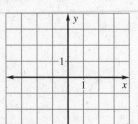

13. $g(x) = x^4 + 2x$

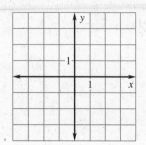

14. $h(x) = -x^4 + 2x^3 - 5x + 1$

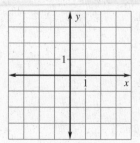

15. Shopping The retail space in shopping centers in the United States from 1986 to 2003 can be modeled by

$$S = -0.0388t^4 + 1.723t^3 - 28t^2 + 309t + 3481$$

where S is the amount of retail space (in millions of square feet) and t is the number of years since 1986.

a. Describe the end behavior of the graph of the function.

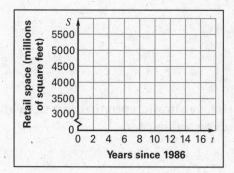

b. Graph the function on the domain $0 \le t \le 17$.

c. Use the graph to estimate the first year that the amount of retail space was greater than 5000 million square feet.

d. Use the model to predict the amount of retail space in the year 2010. Is it appropriate to use the model to make this prediction? *Explain.*

Practice
LESSON 5.3
For use with pages 346–352

Find the sum or difference.

1. $(2y^2 - 5y + 1) + (y^2 - y - 4)$

2. $(12x^2 + 8x - 3) - (11x^2 - x + 5)$

3. $(6m^3 - 5) - (m^3 + 4m^2 - 9m - 2)$

4. $(5s^4 - 2s^3 + 9) - (-2s^4 + 8s^2 - s + 2)$

5. $(7q - 3q^3) + (16 - 8q^3 + 5q^2 - q)$

6. $(-4z^4 + 6z - 9) + (11 - z^3 + 3z^2 + z^4)$

7. $(10v^4 - 2v^2 + 6v^3 - 7) - (9 - v + 2v^4)$

8. $(4x^5 + 3x^4 - 5x + 1) - (x^3 + 2x^4 - x^5 + 1)$

Name _____ Date _____

Find the product.

9. $2x^3(5x - 1)$

10. $(w - 8)(w - 1)$

11. $(c + 4)(c + 10)$

12. $(g + 9)(g - 2)$

13. $(y - 1)(y^2 + 6y - 2)$

14. $(n + 5)(2n^2 - n - 7)$

15. $(x - 3)^2$

16. $(4t + 1)^2$

17. $(z - 5)^3$

18. $(2f + 1)^3$

Write the volume of the figure as a polynomial in standard form.

19. $V = \ell w h$

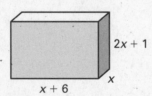

2x + 1

x

x + 6

20. $V = \frac{1}{3}\pi r^2 h$

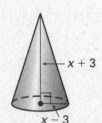

x + 3

x − 3

21. **Bottled Water** From 1990 to 1999, the per person consumption B of bottled water (in gallons) and the population P of the United States (in thousands) can be modeled by

$B = 0.0977t^2 + 0.186t + 7.86$ and

$P = 3226t + 250{,}359$

where t is the number of years since 1990. Write a model for the total consumption C of bottled water (in thousands of gallons). What was the total consumption of bottled water in 1998?

Practice

LESSON 5.4

For use with pages 353–359

Factor the sum or difference of cubes.

1. $x^3 + 125$

2. $y^3 - 8$

3. $64n^3 - 27$

4. $27g^3 + 343$

5. $2w^3 + 54$

6. $40v^3 - 625$

Factor the polynomial by grouping.

7. $r^3 - 3r^2 + 6r - 18$

8. $x^3 + 6x^2 + 7x + 42$

9. $c^3 + 4c^2 - 9c - 36$

10. $z^3 - 2z^2 - 16z + 32$

11. $25p^3 - 25p^2 - p + 1$

12. $9m^3 + 18m^2 - 4m - 8$

Factor the polynomial in quadratic form.

13. $x^4 - 36$

14. $c^4 - 81$

15. $x^4 + x^2 - 20$

16. $6y^6 - 5y^3 - 4$

**LESSON
5.4**   **Practice**   *continued*
For use with pages 353–359

Factor the polynomial completely.

17. $x^6 - 4$

18. $d^4 - 7d^2 + 10$

19. $24q^3 - 81$

20. $a^6 + 7a^3 + 6$

21. $-4x^4 + 26x^2 - 30$

22. $2b^4 + 14b^3 - 16b - 112$

Find the real-number solutions of the equation.

23. $n^4 + 6n^3 = 0$

24. $4k^3 = 9k^2$

25. $x^3 + 2x^2 - 25x - 50 = 0$

26. $6w^3 + 30w^2 - 18w - 90 = 0$

27. $y^4 - 14y^2 + 45 = 0$

28. $3r^5 + 15r^3 - 18r = 0$

29. Write a binomial that can be factored either as the difference of two squares or as the difference of two cubes. Show the complete factorization of your binomial.

30. **City Park** You are designing a marble planter for a city park. You want the length of the planter to be six times the height, and the width to be three times the height. The sides should be one foot thick. Because the planter will be on the sidewalk, it does not need a bottom. What should the outer dimensions of the planter be if it is to hold 4 cubic feet of dirt?

x

$3x$

$6x$

Practice
LESSON 5.5
For use with pages 362–368

Divide using polynomial long division.

1. $(x^2 + 5x - 14) \div (x - 2)$

2. $(x^2 - 2x - 48) \div (x + 5)$

3. $(x^3 + x + 30) \div (x + 3)$

4. $(6x^2 - 5x + 9) \div (2x - 1)$

5. $(8x^3 + 5x^2 - 12x + 10) \div (x^2 - 3)$

6. $(5x^4 + 2x^3 - 9x + 12) \div (x^2 - 3x + 4)$

Divide using synthetic division.

7. $(x^2 + 7x + 12) \div (x + 4)$

8. $(x^3 - 3x^2 + 8x - 5) \div (x - 1)$

9. $(x^4 - 7x^2 + 9x - 10) \div (x - 2)$

10. $(2x^4 - x^3 + 4) \div (x + 1)$

11. $(2x^4 - 11x^3 + 15x^2 + 6x - 18) \div (x - 3)$

12. $(x^4 - 6x^3 - 40x + 33) \div (x - 7)$

A polynomial f and a factor of f are given. Factor f completely.

13. $f(x) = x^3 - 3x^2 - 16x - 12; \ x - 6$

14. $f(x) = x^3 - 12x^2 + 12x + 80; \ x - 10$

15. $f(x) = x^3 - 18x^2 + 95x - 126; \ x - 9$

LESSON 5.5 **Practice** *continued*
For use with pages 362–368

16. $f(x) = x^3 - x^2 - 21x + 45; x + 5$

17. $f(x) = 4x^3 - 4x^2 - 9x + 9; x - 1$

18. $f(x) = 3x^3 - 16x^2 - 103x + 36; x + 4$

A polynomial *f* and one zero of *f* are given. Find the other zeros of *f*.

19. $f(x) = x^3 + 2x^2 - 20x + 24; -6$

20. $f(x) = x^3 + 11x^2 - 150x - 1512; -14$

21. $f(x) = 2x^3 + 3x^2 - 39x - 20; 4$

22. $f(x) = 15x^3 - 119x^2 - 10x + 16; 8$

23. $f(x) = x^3 - 3x^2 - 45x + 175; -7$

24. $f(x) = x^3 - 9x^2 - 5x + 45; 9$

25. **Geometry** The volume of the box shown at the right is given by $V = 2x^3 - 11x^2 + 10x + 8$. Find an expression for the missing dimension.

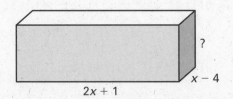

2x + 1

x − 4

?

26. **Fuel Consumption** From 1995 to 2002, the total fuel consumption T (in billions of gallons) by cars in the United States and the U.S. population P (in millions) can be modeled by

$$T = -0.003x^3 - 0.02x^2 + 1.3x + 68 \text{ and } P = 3x + 267$$

where x is the number of years since 1995. Write a function for the average amount of fuel consumed by each person from 1995 to 2002.

LESSON 5.6   **Practice**
For use with pages 370–378

List the possible rational zeros of the function using the rational zero theorem.

1. $f(x) = x^4 - 6x^3 + 8x^2 - 21$

2. $h(x) = 2x^3 + 7x^2 - 7x + 30$

3. $h(x) = 5x^4 + 12x^3 - 16x^2 + 10$

4. $g(x) = 9x^5 + 3x^3 + 7x - 4$

Find all real zeros of the function.

5. $f(x) = x^3 - 3x^2 - 6x + 8$

6. $g(x) = x^3 + 4x^2 - x - 4$

7. $h(x) = x^3 + 4x^2 + x - 6$

8. $g(x) = x^3 + 5x^2 - x - 5$

9. $f(x) = x^3 + 72 - 5x^2 - 18x$

10. $f(x) = x^3 + x^2 - 2x - 2$

Use the graph to shorten the list of possible rational zeros of the function. Then find all real zeros of the function.

11. $f(x) = 4x^3 - 8x^2 - 15x + 9$

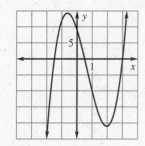

12. $f(x) = 2x^3 - 5x^2 - 4x + 10$

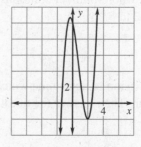

LESSON 5.6

Practice *continued*
For use with pages 370–378

Find all real zeros of the function.

13. $g(x) = 2x^3 + 4x^2 - 2x - 4$

14. $f(x) = 2x^3 - 5x^2 - 14x + 8$

15. $h(x) = 8x^3 - 6x^2 - 23x + 6$

16. $g(x) = 2x^4 + x^3 - x^2 - x - 1$

17. $h(x) = 2x^4 + 5x^3 - 5x^2 - 5x + 3$

18. $f(x) = 2x^4 + 3x^3 - 6x^2 - 6x + 4$

19. Mail From 1995 to 2003, the amount of mail M (in billions of pieces) handled by the U.S. Postal Service can be modeled by

$$M = 0.05(t^4 - 18t^3 + 89t^2 - 32t + 3680)$$

where t is the number of years since 1995. In which year was there about 204,000,000,000 pieces of mail handled?

a. Write a polynomial equation that can be used to answer the question.

b. List the possible whole-number solutions of the equation in part (a) that are less than or equal to 8.

c. Use synthetic division to determine which of the possible solutions in part (b) is an actual solution. Then answer the question in the problem statement.

d. Use a graphing calculator to graph and identify any additional real solutions of the equation that are reasonable.

LESSON 5.7 **Practice**
For use with pages 379–386

Identify the number of solutions or zeros.

1. $f(x) = 5x^3 - 6x^2 + 2x - 3$

2. $g(s) = 8s^6 - 3s^4 - 11s^3 - 2s^2 + 4$

3. $-3y^7 + 5y^5 - 12y + 2 = 6$

4. $4 - 7x = x^2 - 3x^5$

Find all the zeros of the polynomial function.

5. $h(x) = x^3 - 3x^2 - x + 3$

6. $f(x) = x^4 - 4x^3 - 20x^2 + 48x$

7. $g(x) = x^3 + 5x^2 + x + 5$

8. $g(x) = x^4 - 9x^3 + 23x^2 - 81x + 126$

9. $f(x) = x^3 - x^2 - 11x + 3$

10. $h(x) = 2x^4 + x^3 + x^2 + x - 1$

Write a polynomial function *f* of least degree that has rational coefficients, a leading coefficient of 1, and the given zeros.

11. $-7, -4$

12. $1, 2, 5$

13. $-3, 0, 1$

14. $4, i, -i$

15. $-5, 0, -2i, 2i$

16. $8, 2 + i$

Algebra 2

17. Multiple Choice Which is *not* a possible classification of the zeros of $f(x) = x^4 + 2x^3 - 7x^2 - 7x + 3$ according to Descartes' rule of signs?

   A. 2 positive real zeros, 2 negative real zeros, and 0 imaginary zeros

   B. 0 positive real zeros, 2 negative real zeros, and 2 imaginary zeros

   C. 0 positive real zeros, 0 negative real zeros, and 4 imaginary zeros

   D. 1 positive real zero, 1 negative real zero, and 2 imaginary zeros

Use a graphing calculator to graph the function. Then use the *zero* (or *root*) feature to approximate the real zeros of the function.

18. $g(x) = x^3 - x^2 - 5x + 3$

19. $h(x) = 2x^3 - x^2 - 3x - 1$

20. $f(x) = x^4 - 2x - 1$

21. $g(x) = x^4 - x^3 - 20x^2 + 10x + 27$

22. Sporting Goods For 1998 through 2005, the sales S (in billions of dollars) of sporting goods can be modeled by

$$S = 0.007t^3 + 0.1t^2 + 1.4x + 70$$

where t is the number of years since 1998. In which year were sales about $78 billion?

23. Grocery Store Revenue For the 25 years that a grocery store has been open, its annual revenue R (in millions of dollars) can be modeled by

$$R = \frac{1}{10,000}(-t^4 + 12t^3 - 77t^2 + 600t + 13,650)$$

where t is the number of years the store has been open. In what year(s) was the revenue $1.5 million?

LESSON 5.8 **Practice**
For use with pages 387–392

1. Describe and correct the error in the following statement.

If −6 is a solution of the polynomial equation f(x) = 0, then *−6 is a factor of f(x).*

State the maximum number of turns in the graph of the function.

2. $f(x) = x^4 + 2x^2 + 4$ **3.** $f(x) = -3x^3 + x^2 - x + 5$ **4.** $g(x) = 2x^6 + 1$

5. $g(x) = 4x^2 - 5x + 3$ **6.** $h(x) = 3x^7 - 6x^2 + 7$ **7.** $h(x) = 2x^9 - 8x^7 + 7x^5$

Determine the *x*-intercepts of the function.

8. $g(x) = (x + 3)(x - 2)(x - 5)$ **9.** $h(x) = (x + 4)(x - 6)(x - 8)$

10. $f(x) = (x + 3)^2(x - 2)$ **11.** $f(x) = (x + 5)(x + 1)(x - 7)$

12. $g(x) = (x + 6)^3(x + 2)$ **13.** $h(x) = (x - 8)^5$

LESSON 5.8

Practice *continued*
For use with pages 387–392

Graph the function.

14. $f(x) = (x - 3)(x + 2)(x + 1)$

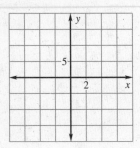

15. $g(x) = (x - 3)^2(x + 2)$

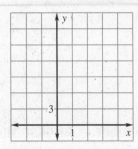

16. $h(x) = 0.3(x + 6)(x - 1)(x - 4)$

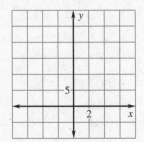

17. $g(x) = \frac{5}{6}(x + 1)^2(x - 1)(x - 4)$

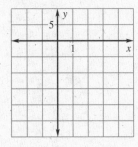

18. $h(x) = (x - 1)(x^2 + x + 1)$

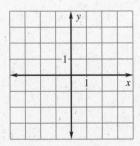

19. $f(x) = (x + 2)(x^2 + 2x + 2)$

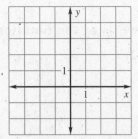

Estimate the coordinates of each turning point and state whether each corresponds to a local maximum or a local minimum. Then estimate all real zeros and determine the least degree the function can have.

20.

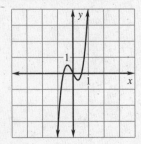

21.

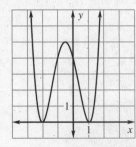

22.

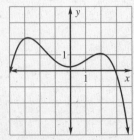

LESSON 5.8 **Practice** *continued*
For use with pages 387–392

Use a graphing calculator to graph the function. Identify the *x*-intercepts and points where local maximums or local minimums occur.

23. $f(x) = 3x^3 - 9x + 1$

24. $h(x) = -\frac{1}{3}x^3 + x - \frac{2}{3}$

25. $g(x) = -\frac{1}{4}x^4 + 2x^2$

26. $f(x) = x^5 - 6x^3 + 9x$

27. $h(x) = x^5 - 5x^3 + 4x$

28. $g(x) = x^4 - 2x^3 - 3x^2 + 5x + 2$

29. Food The average number E of eggs eaten per person each year in the United States from 1970 to 2000 can be modeled by

$$E = 0.000944t^4 - 0.052t^3 + 0.95t^2 - 9.4t + 308$$

where t is the number of years since 1970. Graph the function and identify any turning points on the interval $0 \le t \le 30$. What real-life meaning do these points have?

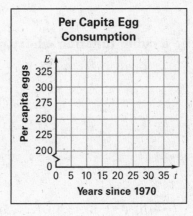

30. Quonset Huts A Quonset hut is a dwelling shaped like half a cylinder. You have 600 square feet of material with which to build a Quonset hut.

   a. The formula for surface area is $S = \pi r^2 + \pi r \ell$ where r is the radius of the semicircle and ℓ is the length of the hut. Substitute 600 for S and solve for ℓ.

   b. The formula for the volume of the hut is $V = \frac{1}{2}\pi r^2 \ell$. Write an equation for the volume V of the Quonset hut as a polynomial function of r by substituting the expression for ℓ from part (a) into the volume formula.

   c. Use the function from part (b) to find the maximum volume of a Quonset hut with a surface area of 600 square feet. What are the hut's dimensions?

LESSON 5.9 **Practice**
For use with pages 393–399

Write the cubic function whose graph is shown.

1.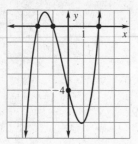

2.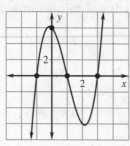

3.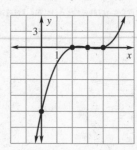

Write a cubic function whose graph passes through the points.

4. $(-2, 0), (0, 0), (1, 0), (2, 1)$

5. $(-4, 0), (-1, 0), (3, 0), (2, -2)$

6. $(-5, 0), (3, 0), (4, 0), (-1, -1)$

7. $(-3, 0), (0, 0), (1, 0), (-2, 4)$

LESSON 5.9 **Practice** *continued*
For use with pages 393–399

Show that the *n*th-order differences for the given function of degree *n* are nonzero and constant.

8. $f(x) = -x^3 + 2x^2 - 1$ **9.** $f(x) = x^4 - 5x^3 + 3$

Use finite differences and a system of equations to find a polynomial function that fits the data.

10.

x	1	2	3	4	5	6
$f(x)$	5	19	49	101	181	295

11.

x	1	2	3	4	5	6
$f(x)$	-5	-6	-1	16	51	110

12. **Space Exploration** The table shows the average speed y (in feet per second) of a space shuttle for different times t (in seconds) after launch.

t	10	20	30	40	50	60	70	80
y	202.4	463.4	748.2	979.3	1186.3	1421.3	1795.4	2283.5

a. Use a graphing calculator to find a polynomial model for the data.

b. When the space shuttle reaches a speed of approximately 4400 feet per second, its booster rockets fall off. Use the model from part (a) to determine how long after launch this happens.

Name _____ Date _____

Rewrite the expression using rational exponent notation.

1. $\sqrt[3]{7}$

2. $\left(\sqrt[3]{6}\right)^2$

3. $\left(\sqrt[5]{14}\right)^4$

4. $\left(\sqrt[7]{-21}\right)^3$

5. $\left(\sqrt[8]{11}\right)^7$

6. $\left(\sqrt[9]{-2}\right)^4$

Rewrite the expression using radical notation.

7. $17^{1/3}$

8. $44^{1/6}$

9. $33^{2/3}$

10. $9^{5/3}$

11. $(-28)^{7/5}$

12. $39^{4/7}$

Evaluate the expression without using a calculator.

13. $\left(\sqrt[3]{8}\right)^2$

14. $\left(\sqrt[4]{16}\right)^3$

15. $\left(\sqrt[4]{81}\right)^4$

16. $36^{3/2}$

17. $4^{5/2}$

18. $27^{2/3}$

19. $125^{4/3}$

20. $(-8)^{1/3}$

21. $(-32)^{3/5}$

Name _____ Date _____

**Graph the function f. Then use the horizontal line test to determine
whether the inverse of f is a function.**

13. $f(x) = 2x + 1$ **14.** $f(x) = -x - 2$ **15.** $f(x) = \frac{1}{2}x^2 - 1$

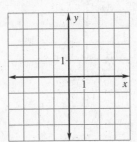   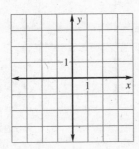   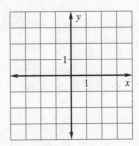

16. $f(x) = -x^2 + 3, x \geq 0$ **17.** $f(x) = \frac{1}{4}x^3$ **18.** $f(x) = |x| + 1$

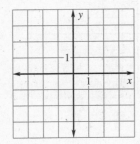   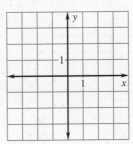   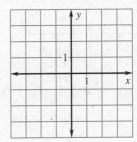

19. Temperature Conversion The formula to convert temperatures from degrees
Celsius to Fahrenheit is $F = \frac{9}{5}C + 32$. Write the inverse function, which converts
temperatures from Fahrenheit to Celsius. What is the Celsius temperature that is
equal to 94 degrees Fahrenheit?

20. Sale Price A department store is having a storewide 20% discount sale. The sale
price S of an item that has a regular price of R is $S = R - 0.2R$. Write the inverse
function. What is the regular price for an item that is on sale for $38.40?

LESSON 6.5 Practice
For use with pages 446–451

Graph the square root function. Then state the domain and range.

1. $f(x) = \sqrt{x} - 2$

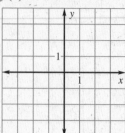

2. $f(x) = \sqrt{x - 2}$

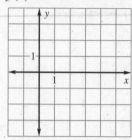

3. $f(x) = 3\sqrt{x + 1}$

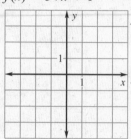

4. $f(x) = \sqrt{x + 2} - 2$

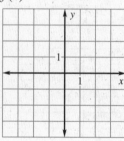

5. $f(x) = \sqrt{x - 1} + 1$

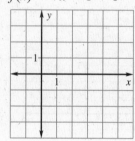

6. $f(x) = -\sqrt{x - 3}$

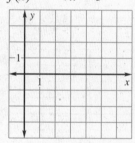

Graph the cube root function. Then state the domain and range.

7. $f(x) = \sqrt[3]{x} + 1$

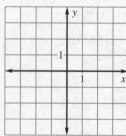

8. $f(x) = \sqrt[3]{x - 4}$

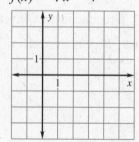

9. $f(x) = 3\sqrt[3]{x}$

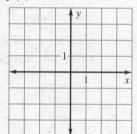

Name _____   Date _____

10. $f(x) = \sqrt[3]{x} + 2$

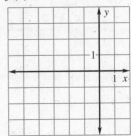

11. $f(x) = -\sqrt[3]{x} - 1$

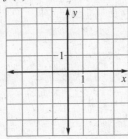

12. $f(x) = \sqrt[3]{x + 2} - 2$

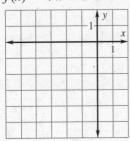

In Exercises 13 and 14, use the following information.

Speed of Sound The speed of sound in feet per second through air of any temperature measured in degrees Celsius is given by $V = \dfrac{1087\sqrt{t + 273}}{16.52}$ where t is the temperature.

13. Identify the domain and range of the function.

14. What is the temperature of the air if the speed of sound is 1250 feet per second?

Name _____ Date _____

 **Practice**
LESSON
6.6
For use with pages 452–459

Solve the equation. Check your solution.

1. $\sqrt{x} + 3 = 12$

2. $x^{1/2} - 4 = 1$

3. $3\sqrt{x + 2} = 6$

4. $(2x - 3)^{1/2} + 2 = 2$

5. $5\sqrt{3x} = 15$

6. $3\sqrt{4 - 3x} = 21$

7. $7 - \sqrt{x - 4} = -6$

8. $\sqrt{3x + 4} + \dfrac{3}{2} = 3$

9. $2(x - 1)^{1/2} - 3 = 7$

Solve the equation. Check your solution.

10. $\sqrt[3]{x} + 1 = -2$

11. $4\sqrt[3]{x} + 2 = 0$

12. $\sqrt[3]{2x + 7} = 5$

13. $(x + 4)^{1/3} - 2 = -6$

14. $8\sqrt[3]{x} + 3 = 11$

15. $3x^{1/3} - 2 = -4$

16. $-2\sqrt[3]{2x + 5} + 7 = 15$

17. $\dfrac{1}{2}(5x + 1)^{1/3} + \dfrac{5}{2} = 4$

18. $6\sqrt[3]{x - 3} + 2 = \dfrac{1}{2}$

Solve the equation. Check for extraneous solutions.

19. $x^{5/3} = 243$

20. $x^{3/2} + 3 = 11$

21. $2x^{5/3} = -64$

22. $(x - 2)^{3/4} = 8$

23. $(2x + 12)^{2/3} - 3 = 13$

24. $(3x + 21)^{4/3} + 9 = 90$

LESSON 7.6 **Practice** *continued*
For use with pages 515–522

Solve the logarithmic equation. Check for extraneous solutions. Round the result to three decimal places if necessary.

28. $\log x = 3$

29. $\ln x = 4$

30. $\log_3 x = 5$

31. $\log_7(2 - x) = \log_7 5x$

32. $\ln(3x - 3) = \ln(x - 6)$

33. $\ln(5 - 2x) = \ln(5x + 3)$

34. $\log_4 3x = 6$

35. $\log_2(3x - 1) = 8$

36. $7 - \log_3 8x = 2$

37. $2 \log_7(1 - 2x) = 12$

38. $3 \ln x - 7 = 4$

39. $\ln(1 - 3x) + 3 = 9$

40. $\log 7x + 4 = 5$

41. $4 + \log_9(3x - 7) = 6$

42. $\log_2 2x + \log_2 x = 5$

43. $\log_6(2x - 6) + \log_6 x = 2$

44. $\ln 3x - \ln 2 = 4$

45. $\ln(-5x + 3) = \ln 2x + 2$

46. **Multiple Choice** You deposit $500 in an account that pays 3.25% annual interest compounded monthly. About how long does it take for the balance to quadruple?

    A. 36.3 years   **B.** 42.7 years   **C.** 45.1 years

In Exercises 47–49, use the following information.

Compounding Interest You deposit $700 in an account that pays 2.75% annual interest. How long does it take the balance to reach the following amounts?

47. $1000 when interest is compounded quarterly

48. $1500 when interest is compounded yearly

49. $2000 when interest is compounded continuously

50. **Rocket Velocity** Disregarding the force of gravity, the maximum velocity v of a rocket is given by $v = t \ln M$ where t is the velocity of the exhaust and M is the ratio of the mass of the rocket with fuel to its mass without fuel. A solid propellant rocket has an exhaust velocity of 2.3 kilometers per second. Its maximum velocity is 7.2 kilometers per second. Find its mass ratio M.

Name _____ Date _____

Write an exponential function $y = ab^x$ whose graph passes through the given points.

1. $\left(0, \dfrac{1}{2}\right), \left(2, \dfrac{9}{2}\right)$ **2.** $\left(1, \dfrac{2}{5}\right), \left(3, \dfrac{8}{5}\right)$ **3.** $(1, 12), \left(-1, \dfrac{3}{4}\right)$

4. $(2, 2), (3, 1)$ **5.** $(0, 5), \left(2, \dfrac{20}{9}\right)$ **6.** $\left(0, \dfrac{3}{4}\right), \left(1, \dfrac{1}{4}\right)$

Find an exponential model by solving for y.

7. $\ln y = 1.924x + 3.634$ **8.** $\ln y = 0.283x - 6.275$ **9.** $\ln y = -3.5x + 4.129$

10. Use the points (x, y) to draw a scatter plot of the points $(x, \ln y)$. Then find an exponential model for the data.

x	1	2	3	4	5	6
y	3.36	9.41	26.34	73.76	206.52	578.27

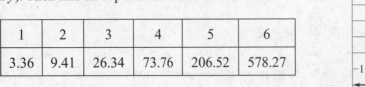

Name _____ Date _____

Write a power function $y = ax^b$ whose graph passes through the given points.

11. $(1, 3), (2, 24)$ **12.** $(1, 0.5), (4, 8)$ **13.** $(1, 2), (4, 16)$

14. $(1, -4), (4, -64)$ **15.** $(4, 0.5), (9, 0.75)$ **16.** $(3, -7.794), (7, -64.82)$

Find a power model by solving for y.

17. $\ln y = 3.3 \ln x + 2.56$ **18.** $\ln y = 1.05 \ln x - 4.28$ **19.** $\ln y = 2 \ln 2x + 3.15$

20. Use the points (x, y) to draw a scatter plot of the points $(\ln x, \ln y)$. Then find a power model for the data.

x	1	2	3	4	5	6
y	2.1	7.313	15.172	25.464	38.051	52.831

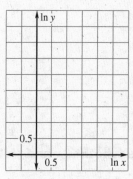

21. **Minimum Wage** The table shows the minimum hourly wage in the United States since 1960. Let $x = 1$ represent the year 1960, $x = 2$ represent the year 1965, and so on. Let y represent the minimum hourly wage. Use a graphing calculator to find a power model for the data. Use the model to estimate the minimum hourly wage in 2020.

Year	1960	1965	1970	1975	1980	1985	1990	1995	2000	2005
Wage	$1.00	$1.25	$1.60	$2.10	$3.10	$3.35	$3.80	$4.25	$5.15	$5.15

Name _____ Date _____

Tell whether *x* and *y* show *direct variation*, *inverse variation*, or *neither*.

1. $y = 2x + 3$ **2.** $y = \dfrac{x}{3}$ **3.** $x = \dfrac{3}{y}$ **4.** $\dfrac{1}{2}xy = 2$

The variables *x* and *y* vary inversely. Use the given values to write an equation relating *x* and *y*. Then find *y* when *x* = 0.5.

5. $x = 4, y = 6$ **6.** $x = 2, y = \dfrac{5}{2}$ **7.** $x = 48, y = \dfrac{1}{12}$

8. $x = -3, y = 2$ **9.** $x = \dfrac{4}{3}, y = \dfrac{3}{2}$ **10.** $x = \dfrac{1}{2}, y = \dfrac{1}{3}$

Determine whether *x* and *y* show *direct variation*, *inverse variation*, or *neither*.

11.

x	1	2	3	4
y	1	4	9	16

12.

x	2	5	8	15
y	60	24	15	8

13.

x	1	4	7	10
y	7.5	30	52.5	75

LESSON 8.1 Practice *continued*
For use with pages 550–557

The variable *z* varies jointly with *x* and *y*. Use the given values to write an equation relating *x*, *y*, and *z*. Then find *z* when *x* = 4 and *y* = 7.

14. $x = 3, y = 5, z = 30$

15. $x = 6, y = \frac{1}{2}, z = 24$

16. $x = \frac{3}{2}, y = 18, z = 9$

In Exercises 17–20, use the following information.

Simple Interest The simple interest I (in dollars) for a savings account is jointly proportional to the product of the time t (in years) and the principal P (in dollars). After fifteen months, the interest on a principal of $2500 is $78.13.

17. Find the constant of variation k.

18. Write an equation that relates I, t, and P.

19. What will the interest I be after ten years?

20. What does the constant of variation k represent?

In Exercises 21–23, use the following information.

Boyle's Law Boyle's Law states that for a constant temperature, the pressure p of a gas varies inversely with its volume V. A sample of oxygen gas has a volume of 50.25 cubic milliliters at a pressure of 20.6 atmospheres.

21. Find the constant of variation k.

22. Write an equation that relates p and V.

23. Find the volume of the oxygen gas if the pressure changes to 15.2 atmospheres.

Name _____ Date _____

Practice

For use with pages 558–564

Find the vertical and horizontal asymptotes of the graph of the function.

1. $f(x) = \dfrac{4}{x-2} + 1$

2. $f(x) = \dfrac{2x+2}{3x-4}$

3. $f(x) = \dfrac{x+1}{2x-3}$

4. $f(x) = \dfrac{4x}{2x+3}$

5. $f(x) = \dfrac{2x-1}{x-2}$

6. $f(x) = \dfrac{6x-1}{3x+6}$

Graph the function. State the domain and range.

7. $f(x) = \dfrac{2}{x+3}$

8. $f(x) = \dfrac{x+1}{x-3}$

9. $f(x) = \dfrac{4x}{2x-1}$

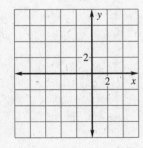

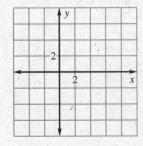

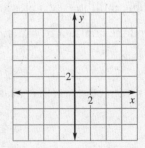

LESSON 8.2 **Practice** *continued*
For use with pages 558–564

10. $f(x) = \dfrac{-3}{x + 2}$

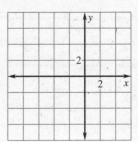

11. $f(x) = \dfrac{3x - 2}{2x + 1}$

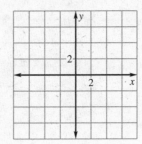

12. $f(x) = \dfrac{4}{3x - 2} - 1$

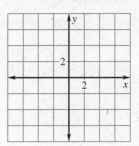

In Exercises 13–16, use the following information.

Phone Bill Your local phone company charges a $65 installation fee and a monthly fee of $32. Let x represent the number of months of phone service.

13. Write an equation that represents the total cost C.

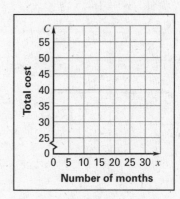

14. Write an equation that represents the average cost A per month.

15. Graph the model in Exercise 14.

16. How many months until the average cost per month is $33.25?

Name _____   Date _____

Identify the *x*-intercept(s) and vertical asymptote(s) of the graph of the function.

1. $y = \dfrac{x^2 + 2x - 15}{x^2 - 36}$

2. $y = \dfrac{x^2 - 2x + 1}{x^2 - 2}$

3. $y = \dfrac{2x - 1}{x^2 + 7}$

Graph the function.

4. $f(x) = \dfrac{2x + 4}{x^2 - 16}$

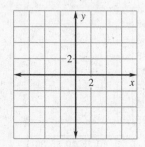

5. $f(x) = \dfrac{2x^2}{x^2 + 5x + 4}$

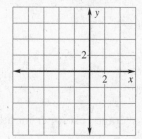

6. $f(x) = \dfrac{x^2 - 3}{2x^2 + 5x - 12}$

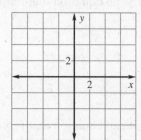

7. $f(x) = \dfrac{x^2 - 25}{x - 4}$

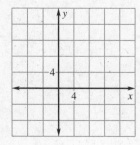

8. $f(x) = \dfrac{5x^2 + 7x + 2}{2x^2 - 8}$

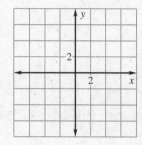

9. $f(x) = \dfrac{2x^2 + 3}{x^3}$

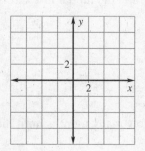

LESSON 8.3 **Practice** *continued*
For use with pages 565–571

10. **Critical Thinking** Give an example of a rational function whose graph has two vertical asymptotes, $x = 6$ and $x = 0$, and does not have any x-intercepts.

In Exercises 11 and 12, use the following information.

Pollution Suppose organic waste was dumped into a pond. Part of the decomposition process includes oxidation, whereby oxygen that is dissolved in the pond water is combined with decomposing material. The oxygen level L in the pond can be modeled by $L = \dfrac{t^2 - t + 1}{t^2 + 1}$ where t represents the number of weeks after the waste is dumped. The normal oxygen level in the pond is $L = 1$.

11. Graph the model for $0 \le t \le 20$.

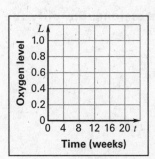

12. Explain how the oxygen level changed during the 20 weeks after the waste was dumped.

LESSON 8.4 **Practice**
For use with pages 573–581

Simplify the rational expression, if possible.

1. $\dfrac{3x - 3}{6}$

2. $\dfrac{(x + 7)(x + 9)}{(x - 9)(x + 7)}$

3. $\dfrac{x + 2}{x^2 - 4x + 4}$

4. $\dfrac{x^2 + 4x - 5}{x^2 - 25}$

5. $\dfrac{x^2 + 4x}{x^2 - 2x - 24}$

6. $\dfrac{x^2 + 10x - 11}{x^2 + 7x - 8}$

Multiply the expressions. Simplify the result.

7. $\dfrac{6x^3y}{xy^2} \cdot \dfrac{3x^2y}{8x^3}$

8. $\dfrac{44x^7y^4}{5xy^2} \cdot \dfrac{12xy^5}{22x^5y^3}$

9. $\dfrac{5x(x - 2)}{(x + 1)(x - 6)} \cdot \dfrac{(x + 1)}{10(x - 2)(x - 1)}$

10. $\dfrac{x^2 + 4x + 3}{x^2 + 5x + 6} \cdot \dfrac{x^2 - 3x - 10}{x^2 + x}$

11. $\dfrac{x^2 - 9x + 20}{x^2 + 9x + 14} \cdot \dfrac{x^2 + 6x + 8}{x^2 - x - 20}$

12. $\dfrac{x^3 - 9x}{x^2 + 6x + 9} \cdot \dfrac{x^3 + 3x^2}{x - 3}$

Algebra 2

Practice *continued*
For use with pages 573–581

Divide the expressions. Simplify the result.

13. $\dfrac{10x^4}{3xy^2} \div \dfrac{6x^2y}{xy^4}$

14. $\dfrac{16x^2y}{81xy^2} \div \dfrac{24x^2y}{54x^3y^3}$

15. $\dfrac{2x^2 + 4x}{x^2 - 4} \div \dfrac{x^2 - 3x + 2}{3x - 6}$

16. $\dfrac{9x^2}{6x - 3} \div \dfrac{3x^2 - 12x}{2x^2 - x}$

17. $\left(x^2 + 9x + 18\right) \div \dfrac{x^2 - 3x - 18}{x^2 - 9x + 18}$

18. $\dfrac{3x^2 + 4x + 1}{x^2 - 4} \div \dfrac{x + 1}{x^2 + 8x + 12}$

19. Geometry In the diagrams below, the length of the edge of the square is twice as long as the radius of the circle. Find the ratio of the area of the circle to the area of the square. Write your answer in simplified form.

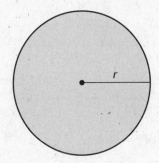

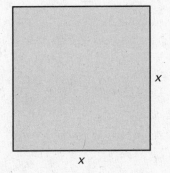

LESSON
8.5 **Practice**
For use with pages 582–588

Find the least common denominator.

1. $\dfrac{2}{x-3}, \dfrac{3}{2x+3}$

2. $\dfrac{8}{x+2}, \dfrac{2x}{x-1}$

3. $\dfrac{3x}{x-2}, \dfrac{2}{x^2-4}$

4. $\dfrac{x}{3x(x+3)}, \dfrac{1}{x^2-9}, \dfrac{4}{x(x-3)}$

Perform the indicated operation and simplify.

5. $\dfrac{2}{3x+1} + \dfrac{x}{3x+1}$

6. $\dfrac{x}{x^2-4x+3} + \dfrac{5}{x-3}$

7. $\dfrac{3x}{x-5} - \dfrac{2}{x^2-25}$

8. $\dfrac{3}{x} + \dfrac{2}{x-2} - \dfrac{2}{x^2}$

9. $\dfrac{x}{x+3} - \dfrac{3}{x+2} - \dfrac{1}{x^2+5x+6}$

10. $\dfrac{2x}{x^2+4x+4} + \dfrac{x-1}{x(x+2)}$

11. $2 + \dfrac{x}{x^2-2}$

12. $\dfrac{x-2}{x^2+x-12} + \dfrac{x}{x^2-2x-3}$

Name _____   Date _____

Simplify the complex fraction.

13. $\dfrac{\dfrac{2}{x} + \dfrac{3}{x-1}}{\dfrac{1}{2x-2}}$

14. $\dfrac{\dfrac{3}{x+2} + \dfrac{2}{3}}{\dfrac{2x}{x+2} - \dfrac{1}{x}}$

15. $\dfrac{\dfrac{3x}{2x-1} - 2}{\dfrac{5}{4x} - \dfrac{x}{2x-1}}$

In Exercises 16 and 17, use the following information.

Doctors Over a twenty year period the number of doctors of medicine M (in thousands) in the United States can be approximated by $M = \dfrac{28{,}390 + 693t}{85 - t}$ where $t = 0$ represents 1980. The number of doctors of osteopathy B (in thousands) can be approximated by $B = \dfrac{776 - 12t}{55 - 2t}$.

16. Write an expression for the total number T of doctors of medicine (MD) and doctors of osteopathy (DO). Simplify the result.

17. How many MDs did the United States have in 1990? how many DOs?

LESSON 8.6 Practice
For use with pages 589–595

Determine whether the given *x*-value is a solution of the equation.

1. $\dfrac{4}{2x-3} + \dfrac{2}{x+4} = \dfrac{2x}{x^2-8}; \ x = \dfrac{3}{2}$

2. $\dfrac{x}{x+4} - \dfrac{2}{x} = \dfrac{2x-8}{x^2}; \ x = 4$

Solve the equation by cross multiplying. Check for extraneous solutions.

3. $2 = \dfrac{x+2}{x-3}$

4. $\dfrac{1}{x+5} = \dfrac{2}{7x}$

5. $\dfrac{x}{3} = \dfrac{-2}{x+7}$

6. $\dfrac{2x+4}{5x} = \dfrac{2}{x}$

7. $\dfrac{x+1}{x-2} = \dfrac{x-3}{x}$

8. $\dfrac{2x+3}{3x} = \dfrac{x}{2x-3}$

9. $\dfrac{x-5}{-3} = \dfrac{4}{x+2}$

10. $\dfrac{2x-6}{x-6} = \dfrac{x}{x+2}$

Solve the equation by using the LCD. Check for extraneous solutions.

11. $\dfrac{3}{2} + \dfrac{1}{x} = 1 + \dfrac{4}{x}$

12. $\dfrac{-x+1}{x-1} + 2 = \dfrac{1}{x}$

13. $1 + \dfrac{6}{x} = \dfrac{2x-4}{x} - 3$

14. $\dfrac{6}{x-3} - 4 = \dfrac{2}{x-3}$

Name _____ Date _____

15. $\dfrac{4}{x-3} + \dfrac{2}{x+3} = \dfrac{2x+2}{x^2-9}$

16. $\dfrac{x^2}{3x-1} + 2 = \dfrac{2(x-3)}{3x-1}$

17. $\dfrac{x}{2x-1} - \dfrac{2}{2x+1} = \dfrac{x^2+20}{4x^2-1}$

18. $x + \dfrac{5}{x+6} = \dfrac{6x-1}{x+6}$

19. Average Cost It costs a manufacturing company $8 to produce one can of paint. If the initial investment in the production line was $50,000, how many cans of paint must be produced before the average cost per can falls to $10?

20. Brakes The braking distance of a car can be modeled by $d = s + \dfrac{s^2}{20}$ where d is the distance (in feet) that the car travels before coming to a stop, and s is the speed at which the car is traveling (in miles per hour). Find the speed that results in a braking distance of 240 feet.

In Exercises 21 and 22, use the following information.

Fuel Efficiency The cost of fueling your car for one year can be calculated using this

equation: Fuel cost for one year $= \dfrac{(\text{Miles driven} \times \text{Price per gallon})}{\text{Fuel efficiency rate}}$

21. Last year you drove 22,500 miles, paid $2.25 per gallon of gasoline, and spent a total of $2025 on gasoline. What is the fuel efficiency rate of your car?

22. How much would you have saved if your car's fuel efficiency rate were 35 miles per gallon?

LESSON 9.1 Practice
For use with pages 614–619

Find the distance between the two points. Then find the midpoint of the line segment joining the two points.

1. $(5, 2), (4, 3)$

2. $(-2, 2), (4, 6)$

3. $(-3, 5), (2, 0)$

4. $(7, 1), (2, 7)$

5. $(5, 5), (-5, 1)$

6. $(9, 3), (1, 1)$

7. $(-7, -8), (2, -4)$

8. $(2.4, 1.2), (1.2, 4.6)$

9. $(0, 6.4), (2.7, 0.8)$

10. $(-3.9, 2.1), (2.7, -2.2)$

11. $\left(\frac{1}{2}, 3\right), \left(\frac{7}{2}, 1\right)$

12. $\left(\frac{2}{3}, -\frac{3}{2}\right), \left(4, \frac{3}{2}\right)$

The vertices of a triangle are given. Classify the triangle as *scalene*, *isosceles*, or *equilateral*.

13. $(2, 7), (4, 4), (-1, -1)$

14. $(-2, 5), (-1, -4), (7, 4)$

15. $(1, 6), (2, 5), (2, 7)\backslash$

Write an equation for the perpendicular bisector of the line segment joining the two points.

16. $(3, 5), (1, 7)$

17. $(7, 5), (1, 2)$

18. $(2, 4), (-3, -6)$

19. $(-2, 1), (-4, -5)$

20. $(8, -4), (6, 4)$

21. $(-1, 3), (4, 1)$

LESSON 9.1 **Practice** *continued*
For use with pages 614–619

Use the given distance *d* between the two points to find the value of *x* or *y*.

22. $(3, 6), (7, y); d = 4\sqrt{2}$

23. $(x, -4), (3, 2); d = 2\sqrt{10}$

24. $(-2, -7), (x, -12); d = \sqrt{89}$

25. $(1, y), (-1, 3); d = 2\sqrt{10}$

In Exercises 26–31, use the following information.

Rival School The center of your hometown is at the origin of the coordinate plane shown. The location of your home, high school, and rival school are also displayed on the coordinate plane. Each unit on the coordinate plane represents two miles. Round your answers to two decimal places.

26. Determine the coordinates of your home.

27. Determine the coordinates of your high school.

28. Determine the coordinates of your rival school.

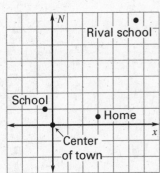

29. Approximate the distance from home to the high school.

30. Approximate the distance from your high school to the rival school.

31. On Friday night, you decide to attend the football game because your school is playing the rival school. It's an away game so you have to drive to the game from home. How long (in minutes) will it take to drive to the rival school if you average 35 miles per hour?

LESSON
9.2   **Practice**
For use with pages 620–625

Tell whether the parabola opens *up*, *down*, *left*, or *right*.

1. $x^2 = -4y$

2. $y^2 = 7x$

3. $y^2 = -2x$

Graph the equation. Identify the focus and directrix of the parabola.

4. $x^2 = 12y$

5. $y^2 = -4x$

6. $x^2 = -y$

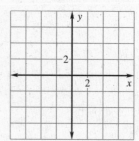

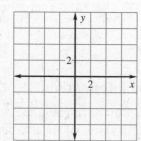

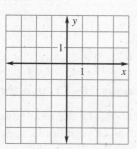

7. $y^2 - 6x = 0$

8. $x^2 + 8y = 0$

9. $2x^2 - y = 0$

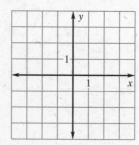

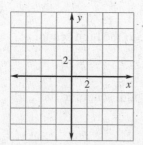

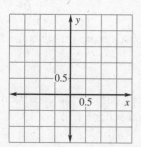

Name _____ Date _____

Write the standard form of the equation of the parabola with the given focus and vertex at (0, 0).

10. $(2, 0)$ **11.** $(0, 1)$ **12.** $(-1, 0)$

13. $\left(0, \dfrac{1}{2}\right)$ **14.** $(3, 0)$ **15.** $(0, -6)$

Write the standard form of the equation of the parabola with the given directrix and vertex at (0, 0).

16. $x = 3$ **17.** $y = -2$ **18.** $x = -1$

19. $y = 4$ **20.** $x = \dfrac{1}{4}$ **21.** $y = -\dfrac{1}{2}$

22. Television Antenna Dish The cross section of a television antenna dish is a parabola. The receiver is located at the focus, 2.5 feet above the vertex. Assume the vertex is at the origin. Write an equation for the cross section of the dish.

23. Headlight The filament of a light bulb is a thin wire that glows when electricity passes through it. The filament of a car headlight is at the focus of a parabolic reflector, which sends light out in a straight beam. Given that the filament is 1.5 inches from the vertex, write an equation for the cross section of the reflector.

LESSON 9.3 **Practice**
For use with pages 626–633

Graph the equation. Identify the radius of the circle.

1. $x^2 + y^2 = 9$

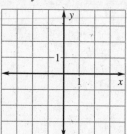

2. $x^2 + y^2 = 20$

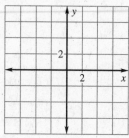

3. $x^2 + y^2 = 64$

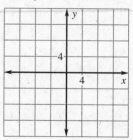

4. $x^2 + y^2 = 50$

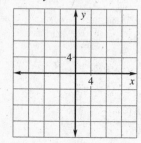

5. $5x^2 + 5y^2 = 80$

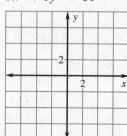

6. $3x^2 + 3y^2 = 120$

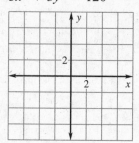

Write the standard form of the equation of the circle with the given radius and whose center is the origin.

7. $\sqrt{7}$

8. $2\sqrt{5}$

9. $3\sqrt{10}$

LESSON 9.3 **Practice** *continued*
For use with pages 626–633

Write the standard form of the equation of the circle that passes through the given point and whose center is the origin.

10. $(2, 3)$

11. $(-3, 5)$

12. $(4, -6)$

The equations of both circles and parabolas are given. Graph the equation.

13. $x^2 + 3y = 0$

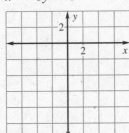

14. $2x^2 + 2y^2 = 8$

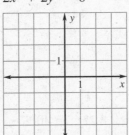

15. $x^2 - 8y = 0$

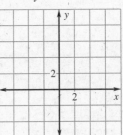

Write an equation of the line tangent to the given circle at the given point.

16. $x^2 + y^2 = 17; (1, 4)$

17. $x^2 + y^2 = 52; (-4, 6)$

18. Capitol Dome The Capitol Dome sits atop the Capitol Building in Washington, D.C. The base of the dome is circular with a diameter of 96 feet. Suppose a coordinate plane was placed over the base of the dome with the origin at the center of the dome. Write an equation in standard form for the outside boundary of the dome.

LESSON 9.4 **Practice**
For use with pages 634–639

Graph the equation. Identify the vertices, co-vertices, and foci of the ellipse.

1. $\dfrac{x^2}{16} + \dfrac{y^2}{36} = 1$

2. $\dfrac{x^2}{49} + \dfrac{y^2}{4} = 1$

3. $\dfrac{x^2}{64} + \dfrac{y^2}{100} = 1$

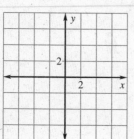
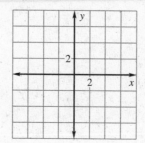
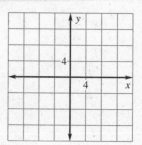

4. $9x^2 + 4y^2 = 36$

5. $16x^2 + 25y^2 = 400$

6. $4x^2 + 81y^2 = 324$

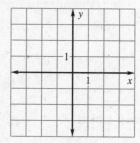
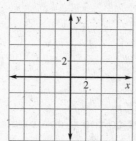
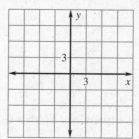

Write an equation of the ellipse with the given characteristics and center at (0, 0).

7. Vertex: $(3, 0)$
Co-vertex: $(0, 2)$

8. Vertex: $(0, 5)$
Co-vertex: $(1, 0)$

9. Vertex: $(-6, 0)$
Co-vertex: $(0, -3)$

Algebra 2
Chapter 9 Practice Workbook

LESSON 9.4 **Practice** *continued*
For use with pages 634–639

10. Vertex: $(0, 4)$

Focus: $(0, 2\sqrt{3})$

11. Vertex: $(-7, 0)$

Focus: $(2\sqrt{6}, 0)$

12. Co-vertex: $(0, 6)$

Focus: $(-2\sqrt{7}, 0)$

The equations of a parabola, a circle, and an ellipse are given. Graph the equation.

13. $x^2 + 12y = 0$

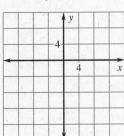

14. $3x^2 + 3y^2 = 48$

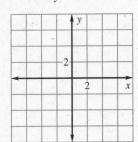

15. $6x^2 + 8y^2 = 96$

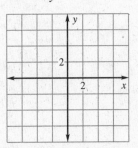

16. Swimming Pool An elliptical pool is 20 feet long and 16 feet wide. Write an equation for the perimeter of the swimming pool. Assume the major axis of the pool is vertical.

17. Race Track The shape of a dirt race track for car racing is approximately an ellipse. The track is 400 feet long and 250 feet wide. Write an equation for the perimeter of the race track. Assume the major axis of the track is horizontal.

Name _____ Date _____

Graph the equation. Identify the vertices, foci, and asymptotes of the hyperbola.

1. $\dfrac{x^2}{16} - \dfrac{y^2}{4} = 1$

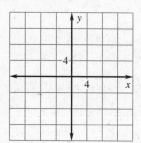

2. $\dfrac{x^2}{9} - \dfrac{y^2}{36} = 1$

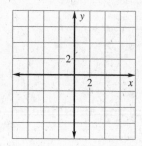

3. $\dfrac{y^2}{25} - \dfrac{x^2}{4} = 1$

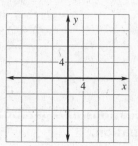

4. $x^2 - 4y^2 = 4$

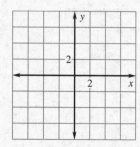

5. $2y^2 - 10x^2 = 40$

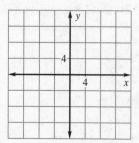

6. $16y^2 - 4x^2 = 64$

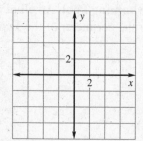

LESSON 9.5 **Practice** *continued*
For use with pages 642–648

Write an equation of the hyperbola with the given foci and vertices.

7. Foci: $(6, 0)$, $(-6, 0)$

Vertices: $(4, 0)$, $(-4, 0)$

8. Foci: $(0, 8)$, $(0, -8)$

Vertices: $(0, 7)$, $(0, -7)$

9. Foci: $(\sqrt{13}, 0)$, $(-\sqrt{13}, 0)$

Vertices: $(2, 0)$, $(-2, 0)$

10. Foci: $(0, \sqrt{61})$, $(0, -\sqrt{61})$

Vertices: $(0, 6)$, $(0, -6)$

The equations of a parabola, an ellipse, and a hyperbola are given. Graph the equation.

11. $25x^2 + 4y^2 = 100$

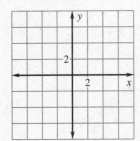

12. $25x^2 + 4y = 0$

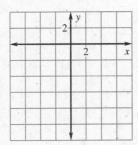

13. $25x^2 - 4y^2 = 100$

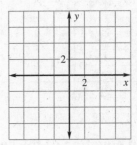

14. Machine Shop A machine shop needs to make a small automotive part by drilling four holes of radius r from a flat circular piece of radius R. The area of the resulting part is eight square inches. Write an equation that relates r and R.

Name _____ Date _____

Graph the equation. Identify the important characteristics of the graph.

1. $x^2 + (y - 3)^2 = 9$

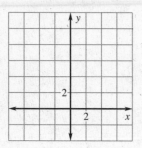

2. $\dfrac{(x - 4)^2}{16} + \dfrac{(y - 2)^2}{4} = 1$

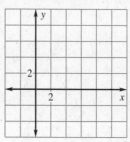

3. $(x - 3)^2 = 8(y + 4)$

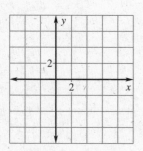

4. $\dfrac{(y + 2)^2}{18} - \dfrac{(x + 1)^2}{25} = 1$

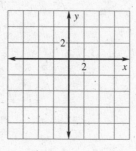

5. $\dfrac{(x + 3)^2}{32} + \dfrac{(y - 4)^2}{36} = 1$

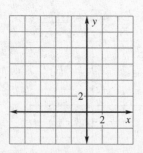

6. $(x - 5)^2 + (y + 2)^2 = 28$

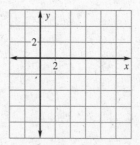

Write an equation of the conic section.

7. Circle with a center at $(2, -6)$ and a radius of 4

8. Parabola with vertex $(3, 3)$ and focus at $(3, 0)$

9. Ellipse with vertices at $(-2, -1)$ and $(-2, 7)$ and co-vertices at $(-4, 3)$ and $(0, 3)$

10. Hyperbola with vertices at $(2, 4)$ and $(8, 4)$ and foci at $(-2, 4)$ and $(12, 4)$

LESSON 9.6 **Practice** *continued*
For use with pages 649–657

Identify the line(s) of symmetry for the conic section.

11. $(y - 2)^2 = 16(x - 6)$

12. $(x - 3)^2 + (y + 4)^2 = 48$

13. $\dfrac{(x - 7)^2}{81} + \dfrac{y^2}{62} = 1$

14. $\dfrac{(y + 5)^2}{24} - (x - 3)^2 = 1$

Use the discriminant to classify the conic section.

15. $2x^2 + 5x + y + 14 = 0$

16. $4x^2 + 4y^2 - 6x + 8y - 10 = 0$

17. $5x^2 - 5y^2 + 4x - 3y + 4 = 0$

18. $x^2 + 4y^2 - 8x - 12y - 2 = 0$

Classify the conic section and write its equation in standard form. Then graph the equation.

19. $y^2 + 8x - 2y - 15 = 0$

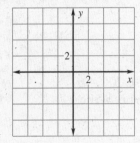

20. $x^2 + y^2 - 12x + 2y + 15 = 0$

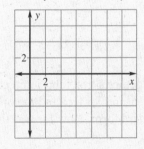

LESSON 9.6
Practice *continued*
For use with pages 649–657

21. $x^2 - 9y^2 + 54y - 90 = 0$

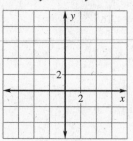

22. $9x^2 + 36y^2 + 54x - 144y - 99 = 0$

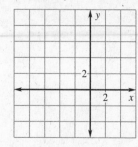

23. $x^2 + 10x - 6y + 7 = 0$

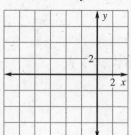

24. $-2x^2 + 5y^2 + 24x - 20y - 102 = 0$

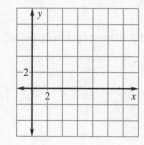

25. Designing a Menu As part of the graphics art department, your job is to create various art pieces and graphical models for your documents. Your newest project is to design a menu that incorporates the picture of a tree. The equation used to model the tree trunk is $9x^2 - y^2 + 8y - 52 = 0$. Write this equation in standard form and then graph the equation.

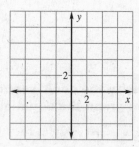

26. Long Jump A competitor's first long jump can be modeled by $x^2 - 20x + 20y = 0$ where x and y are measured in feet and the origin marks the start of the jump. Write the equation in standard form. How far was the first jump?

LESSON 9.7 **Practice**
For use with pages 658–664

Solve the system using a graphing calculator.

1. $x^2 + (y - 3)^2 - 9 = 0$
$x + y - 1 = 0$

2. $2x^2 - y^2 + 4x - 6 = 0$
$2x + y + 4 = 0$

3. $x^2 - y - 4x + 2 = 0$
$x - 2y + 4 = 0$

4. $6x^2 + y^2 = 12$
$3x + y = 1$

5. $(x - 2)^2 + y^2 = 16$
$x = 6$

6. $x - 2x^2 - 3y = 1$
$9x^2 + 4y^2 = 36$

7. Multiple Choice Which ordered pair is a solution of the linear-quadratic system below?

$x^2 - 4x + 4y^2 - 8y = 8$
$2x + y = 7$

A. $(1, 5)$ **B.** $(5, -1)$ **C.** $(2, 3)$ **D.** $(-3, 2)$

Solve the system using substitution.

8. $x^2 + y^2 = 45$
$y = 2x$

9. $x^2 - 3y - 3 = 0$
$x - y = 1$

10. $x^2 - 2x + y^2 - 2y = 2$
$x + y = 4$

11. $-x^2 + 2y^2 = 16$
$x - y = 0$

12. $3x + y^2 + 2 = 0$
$3x = y - 2$

13. $2x^2 + 6y^2 = 18$
$x + 4y + 8 = 0$

14. $2x^2 + y - 3 = 0$
$3x + y = -6$

15. $4x^2 - x - y^2 + 6 = 0$
$2x - y = 3$

16. $2x + y^2 - 4y + 4 = 0$
$-x + y = 2$

LESSON
9.7

Practice *continued*
For use with pages 658–664

Solve the system.

17. $x^2 - y^2 + 4x - 4 = 0$
$-x^2 + y^2 - 3x + 3 = 0$

18. $x^2 + 2y^2 - 3y = 0$
$x^2 + y^2 - 2 = 0$

19. $2x^2 - y^2 - x - 4 = 0$
$-x^2 + y^2 + 3x - 4 = 0$

20. $2x^2 + 3y^2 = 1$
$x^2 + y^2 + 4 = 0$

21. Farming A farmer has 1400 feet of fence to enclose a rectangular area that borders a river. No fence is needed along the river. Is it possible for the farmer to enclose five acres? (1 acre = 43,560 square feet) If possible, find the dimensions of the enclosure.

22. Radio The range of a radio station is bounded by a circle given by the equation $x^2 + y^2 = 920$ where x and y are measured in miles. A straight highway that passes through the area can be modeled by the equation $y = \frac{1}{2}x + 20$. Find the length of the highway that lies within the range of the radio station.

Name _____   Date _____

Each event can occur in the given number of ways. Find the number of ways all of the events can occur.

1. Event 1: 3 ways; Event 2: 7 ways

2. Event 1: 8 ways; Event 2: 5 ways

3. Event 1: 4 ways; Event 2: 2 ways; Event 3: 9 ways

4. Event 1: 6 ways; Event 2: 7 ways; Event 3: 4 ways

For the given configuration, determine how many different computer passwords are possible if (a) digits and letters can be repeated, and (b) digits and letters cannot be repeated.

5. 3 digits followed by 4 letters

6. 2 digits followed by 5 letters

7. 1 letter followed by 6 digits

8. 4 letters followed by 4 digits

Evaluate the expression.

9. 5!

10. 10!

11. 9!

12. 14!

13. 5(3!)

14. 4! · 6!

15. $\dfrac{7!}{3! \cdot 2!}$

16. $\dfrac{11!}{(6+2)!}$

LESSON 10.1 Practice *continued*
For use with pages 682–689

Find the number of permutations.

17. $_4P_3$ **18.** $_7P_5$ **19.** $_8P_4$ **20.** $_9P_0$

21. $_{10}P_3$ **22.** $_9P_6$ **23.** $_{14}P_7$ **24.** $_{12}P_{12}$

Find the number of distinguishable permutations of the letters in the word.

25. MATH   **26.** SOUTH   **27.** BALL   **28.** ODD

29. SPANISH   **30.** MINNESOTA   **31.** DELAWARE   **32.** LETTERS

33. Men's Suits A men's department store sells 3 different suit jackets, 6 different shirts, 8 different ties, and 4 different pairs of pants. How many different suits consisting of a jacket, shirt, tie, and pants are possible?

34. Batting Order A baseball manager is determining the batting order for the team. The team has 9 players, but the manager definitely wants the pitcher to bat last. How many batting orders are possible?

35. Chore Your chores for the week are to cut the grass, wash the car, clean your room, clean the garage, and shine your shoes. You are to do 1 chore each day from Monday through Friday. You can do each chore on whatever day you want, except that you must wash the car either Thursday or Friday. In how many different orders can you perform your chores?

Copyright © by McDougal Littell, a division of Houghton Mifflin Company.

Practice
For use with pages 690–697

Find the number of combinations.

1. $_6C_4$ 2. $_8C_5$ 3. $_7C_3$ 4. $_9C_7$

5. $_{13}C_9$ 6. $_{10}C_6$ 7. $_{12}C_8$ 8. $_{14}C_{10}$

Find the number of possible 5-card hands that contain the cards specified. The cards are taken from a standard 52-card deck.

9. 5 red cards

10. 4 spades and 1 card that is not a spade

11. 3 face cards (kings, queens, or jacks) and 2 cards that are not face cards

12. 2 aces and 3 cards that are not aces

13. At most 1 diamond

14. At least 1 king

Use the binomial theorem to write the binomial expansion.

15. $(x - 2)^4$ 16. $(x + 3)^3$ 17. $(2x + 5)^5$ 18. $(4x - 1)^6$

19. $(x + 6y)^3$ 20. $(x - 5y)^5$ 21. $(3x - y)^6$ 22. $(8x + y)^4$

LESSON 10.2 **Practice** *continued*
For use with pages 690–697

23. Find the coefficient of x^6 in the expansion of $(2x + 3)^{10}$.

24. Find the coefficient of x^4 in the expansion of $(3x - 1)^{11}$.

25. Find the coefficient of x^7 in the expansion of $(2x - 5)^9$.

26. Find the coefficient of x^3 in the expansion of $(3x + 2)^{12}$.

27. **School Play** A teacher is holding tryouts for the school play. There are 15 students trying out for 7 parts in the play. Each student can play each part. In how many ways can the teacher select the students?

28. **Soccer Starters** A youth indoor soccer team has 6 starting players. The starting players must consist of 3 boys and 3 girls. There are 7 boys and 6 girls on the team. Each player can play each position. In how many ways can the coach select players to start the game?

29. **Football Cards** You have a plastic sheet that holds 9 trading cards. You want to fill the sheet with football cards consisting of 4 quarterbacks, 3 running backs, and 2 wide receivers. In your collection of cards, you have 10 quarterbacks, 7 running backs, and 8 wide receivers. In how many different ways can you select the cards?

Algebra 2

LESSON 10.3 Practice
For use with pages 698–704

You have an equally likely chance of choosing any integer from 1 through 80. Find the probability of the given event.

1. An odd number is chosen.

2. A number greater than 50 is chosen.

3. A perfect square is chosen.

4. A perfect cube is chosen.

5. A multiple of 3 is chosen.

6. A factor of 200 is chosen.

7. An even number greater than 30 is chosen.

8. An odd number less than 70 is chosen.

You are rolling a 20-sided die where the sides are numbered 1 through 20. Find the indicated odds.

9. In favor of rolling a 10

10. In favor of rolling a number less than 6

11. Against rolling a 1, 3, or 5

12. Against rolling a number greater than 13

13. In favor of rolling an even number less than 10

14. Against rolling an odd number greater than 10

Practice *continued*
For use with pages 698–704

Find the probability that a dart thrown at the square target shown will hit the given region. Assume the dart is equally likely to hit any point inside the target. Round your answer to three decimal places.

15. The center *a*

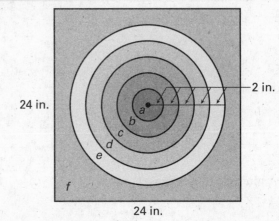

24 in.

2 in.

24 in.

16. The border *f*

17. The center *a* or the ring *b*

18. The four rings (*b*, *c*, *d*, and *e*) or the center *a*

19. The ring *d* or *e*

20. **Flag Carriers** Six students of different heights are going to march in single file in a parade carrying flags. The order in which they march is to be randomly selected. What is the probability that they will march in order of height from shortest to tallest? Round your answer to six decimal places.

Name _____   Date _____

LESSON 10.4
Practice
For use with pages 706–713

Events *A* and *B* are disjoint. Find *P*(*A* or *B*).

1. $P(A) = 0.1$, $P(B) = 0.45$ **2.** $P(A) = 0.85$, $P(B) = 0.05$ **3.** $P(A) = \frac{1}{2}$, $P(B) = \frac{1}{5}$

Find the indicated probability.

4. $P(A) = \frac{1}{6}$, $P(B) = \frac{5}{6}$

$P(A \text{ or } B) = \frac{1}{3}$

$P(A \text{ and } B) = \underline{\ ?\ }$

5. $P(A) = 0.23$, $P(B) = 0.36$

$P(A \text{ or } B) = 0.25$

$P(A \text{ and } B) = \underline{\ ?\ }$

6. $P(A) = \frac{5}{8}$, $P(B) = \frac{1}{4}$

$P(A \text{ or } B) = \frac{1}{2}$

$P(A \text{ and } B) = \underline{\ ?\ }$

Find *P*($\overline{A}$).

7. $P(A) = 1$ **8.** $P(A) = 0.25$ **9.** $P(A) = \frac{9}{16}$

Find the indicated probability. State whether *A* and *B* are disjoint events.

10. $P(A) = \frac{2}{13}$, $P(B) = \underline{\ ?\ }$

$P(A \text{ or } B) = \frac{8}{13}$

$P(A \text{ and } B) = \frac{4}{13}$

11. $P(A) = 17\%$, $P(B) = 35\%$

$P(A \text{ or } B) = 52\%$

$P(A \text{ and } B) = \underline{\ ?\ }$

12. $P(A) = \frac{5}{6}$, $P(B) = \frac{2}{5}$

$P(A \text{ or } B) = \underline{\ ?\ }$

$P(A \text{ and } B) = \frac{2}{3}$

LESSON
10.4

Practice continued
For use with pages 706–713

Two six-sided dice are rolled. Find the probability of the given event.
(Refer to Example 4 on page 709 of the textbook for the possible outcomes.)

13. The sum is greater than 4.

14. The sum is 6 or 11.

15. The sum is neither 5 nor 9.

16. The sum is greater than 7 and less than 11.

17. **Honors Banquet** Of the 120 students honored at an academic banquet, 40% won awards for mathematics and 55% for English. Fourteen of these students won awards for both mathematics and English. One of the 120 students is chosen at random to be interviewed for a newspaper article. What is the probability that the student won an award in mathematics or English?

18. **Parakeets** A pet store has 18 light green parakeets (5 females and 13 males) and 25 sky blue parakeets (15 females and 10 males). You randomly choose one of the parakeets. What is the probability that it is a male or a sky blue parakeet?

19. **Potluck Dinner** The organizer of a potluck dinner sends 6 people a list of 10 different recipes and asks each person to bring one of the items on the list. If all 6 people randomly choose a recipe from the list, what is the probability that at least 2 will bring the same thing?

LESSON 10.5 Practice
For use with pages 717–723

Events *A* and *B* are independent. Find the indicated probability.

1. $P(A) = \dfrac{5}{8}$

$P(B) = \dfrac{4}{5}$

$P(A \text{ and } B) = \underline{}$

2. $P(A) = \underline{}$

$P(B) = 0.3$

$P(A \text{ and } B) = 0.3$

3. $P(A) = 0.9$

$P(B) = \underline{}$

$P(A \text{ and } B) = 0.54$

Events *A* and *B* are dependent. Find the indicated probability.

4. $P(A) = 0.4$

$P(B \mid A) = 0.4$

$P(A \text{ and } B) = \underline{}$

5. $P(A) = \underline{}$

$P(B \mid A) = 0.6$

$P(A \text{ and } B) = 0.15$

6. $P(A) = 0.3$

$P(B \mid A) = \underline{}$

$P(A \text{ and } B) = 0.27$

Let *n* be a randomly selected integer from 1 to 40. Find the indicated probability.

7. *n* is prime given that it is even.

8. *n* is 15 given that it is a multiple of 3.

9. *n* is 32 given that it is greater than 25.

10. *n* is 13 given that it is odd.

LESSON 10.5 **Practice** *continued*
For use with pages 717–723

Find the probability of drawing the given cards from a standard deck of 52 cards (a) with replacement and (b) without replacement.

11. A club, then a diamond

12. A jack, then a 7

13. A 5, then a face card, then an ace

14. A king, then another king, then a third king

In Exercises 15–17, use the following information.

File Cabinet Each drawer in a 5-drawer file cabinet has 50 folders. You are searching for some information that is in one of the folders, but you do not know which folder has the information.

15. What is the probability that the information is in the first drawer you choose?

16. What is the probability that the information is not in the first folder you choose?

17. What is the probability that the information is not in the first six folders you choose?

18. **Apples** The probability of selecting a rotten apple from a basket is 14%. What is the probability of selecting 3 good apples when selecting 1 apple from each of 3 different baskets?

Name _____ Date _____

 LESSON 10.6 Practice
For use with pages 724–731

Calculate the probability of tossing a coin 25 times and getting the given number of heads.

1. 2   **2.** 10   **3.** 18   **4.** 25

Calculate the probability of randomly guessing the given number of correct answers on a 20-question multiple choice exam that has choices A, B, C, and D for each question.

5. 10   **6.** 8   **7.** 18   **8.** 5

Calculate the probability of k successes for a binomial experiment consisting of n trials with probability p of success on each trial.

9. $k \geq 4, n = 8, p = 0.16$ **10.** $k \leq 5, n = 10, p = 0.45$

11. $k \geq 3, n = 5, p = 0.34$ **12.** $k \leq 8, n = 12, p = 0.60$

Practice *continued*
For use with pages 724–731

A binomial experiment consists of *n* trials with probability *p* of success on each trial. Draw a histogram of the binomial distribution that shows the probability of exactly *k* successes. *Describe* the distribution as either *symmetric* or *skewed*. Then find the most likely number of successes.

13. $n = 4, p = 0.45$ **14.** $n = 5, p = 0.75$ **15.** $n = 6, p = 0.83$

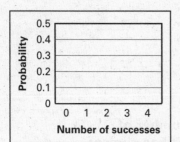
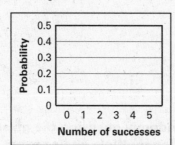
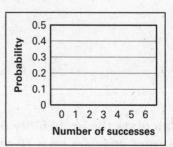

In Exercises 16 and 17, use the following information.

Puppies A registered golden retriever has a litter of 11 puppies. Assume that the probability of a puppy being male is 0.5.

16. Because the owner of the dog can expect to get more money for a male puppy, what is the most likely number of males in the litter?

17. What is the probability at least 7 of the puppies will be male?

Algebra 2

LESSON 11.1 **Practice**
For use with pages 744–750

Find the mean, median, and mode of the data set.

1. 6, 22, 4, 15, 10, 8, 8, 7, 14, 20

2. 10, 15, 12, 20, 25, 22, 28, 24, 22, 26

3. 53, 52, 48, 44, 60, 48, 44, 57, 44

4. 100, 150, 100, 130, 125, 135, 140, 145, 100

Find the range and standard deviation of the data set.

5. 47, 18, 65, 28, 43, 18

6. 70, 27, 41, 30, 10, 47, 11

7. 29.4, 22.9, 15.7, 26.9, 24.0, 27.5, 11.4

8. 35.8, 29.4, 32.1, 24.9, 30.5, 20.3

Identify the outlier in the data set. Then find the mean, median, mode, range, and standard deviation of the data set when the outlier is included and when it is not.

9. 4, 6, 10, 2, 90, 3, 10, 5, 1

10. 52, 61, 55, 1, 59, 68, 69, 55

In Exercises 11–14, find the mean, median, mode, range, and standard deviation of the data set.

11. Cordless Phones The data set below gives the prices (in dollars) of cordless phones at an electronic store.

35, 50, 60, 60, 75, 65, 80

12. Baseball The data set below gives the numbers of homeruns for the 10 batters who hit the most homeruns during the 2005 Major League Baseball regular season.

51, 48, 47, 46, 45, 43, 41, 40, 40, 39

LESSON 11.1 **Practice** *continued*
For use with pages 744–750

13. **Department of Motor Vehicles** The data set below gives the waiting times (in minutes) of several people at a department of motor vehicles service center.

    11, 7, 14, 2, 8, 13, 3, 6, 10, 3, 8, 4, 8, 4, 7

14. **Cereal** The data set below gives the calories in a 1-ounce serving of several breakfast cereals.

    135, 115, 120, 110, 110, 100, 105, 110, 125

In Exercises 15–17, use the following information.

High Temperatures The data set below gives a city's high temperatures (in degrees Fahrenheit) during a 15-day period.

36, 37, 36, 34, 49, 33, 30, 30, 32, 31, 31, 32, 32, 33, 35

15. Identify the outlier in the data set.

16. Find the mean, median, mode, range, and standard deviation of the data set when the outlier is included and when it is not.

17. *Describe* the outlier's effect on the measures of central tendency and dispersion.

LESSON 11.2 **Practice**
For use with pages 751–755

Find the mean, median, mode, range, and standard deviation of the given data set and of the data set obtained by adding the given constant to each data value.

1. 25, 13, 19, 20, 19, 16, 15; constant: 5   **2.** 40, 48, 44, 40, 35, 47, 36; constant: 16

3. 89, 87, 76, 66, 93, 66, 85, 67; constant: 19   **4.** 177, 203, 185, 202, 179, 185; constant: 135

5. 55, 59, 52, 65, 56, 59, 58; constant: −26   **6.** 318, 306, 306, 314, 310, 319; constant: −52

Find the mean, median, mode, range, and standard deviation of the given data set and of the data set obtained by multiplying each data value by the given constant.

7. 19, 25, 28, 20, 27, 8, 25; constant: 2

8. 64, 69, 68, 71, 73, 64, 73; constant: 5

9. 27, 24, 26, 30, 34, 30, 18; constant: 1.1

10. 100, 101, 101, 105, 99, 104, 102; constant: 2.2

11. 150, 156, 163, 156, 165, 155; constant: 0.4

12. 287, 297, 301, 287, 283, 298; constant: 0.7

LESSON
11.2

Practice *continued*
For use with pages 751–755

In Exercises 13 and 14, use the following information.

Test Scores The data set below gives the test scores of several students.

92, 97, 95, 93, 84, 85, 92, 87, 100, 94

13. Find the mean, median, mode, range, and standard deviation of the test scores.

14. Each student receives 10 points for correctly answering a bonus question. Find the mean, median, mode, range, and standard deviation of the test scores including the bonus points.

In Exercises 15 and 16, use the following information.

Auto Batteries The data set below gives the prices (in dollars) of auto batteries at an auto parts store.

80, 60, 65, 90, 45, 55, 70, 55, 65, 90, 65

15. Find the mean, median, mode, range, and standard deviation of the prices.

16. The store has a sale in which all auto batteries are 20% off. Find the mean, median, mode, range, and standard deviation of the sale prices.

Practice

11.3 *For use with pages 757–762*

A normal distribution has mean $\bar{x}$ and standard deviation σ. Find the indicated probability for a randomly selected x-value from the distribution.

1. $P(x \geq \bar{x} + \sigma)$ **2.** $P(x \leq \bar{x} + 2\sigma)$ **3.** $P(x \geq \bar{x} - 3\sigma)$

Give the percent of the area under the normal curve represented by the shaded region.

4.

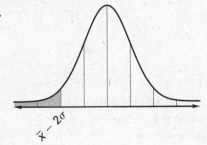

5.

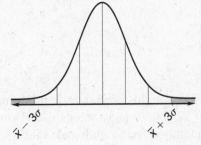

A normal distribution has a mean of 27 and a standard deviation of 5. Find the probability that a randomly selected x-value from the distribution is in the given interval.

6. Between 22 and 32   **7.** Between 12 and 27   **8.** Between 17 and 37

9. At least 22   **10.** At least 37   **11.** At most 32

LESSON
11.3

Practice   *continued*
For use with pages 751–755

A normal distribution has a mean of 75 and a standard deviation of 10.
Use the standard normal table on page 759 of your textbook to find the
indicated probability for a randomly selected *x*-value from the distribution.

12. $P(x \le 70)$ **13.** $P(x \le 52)$ **14.** $P(x \le 78)$

15. $P(x \le 96)$ **16.** $P(x \le 44)$ **17.** $P(x \le 106)$

18. Biology The weights of adult male rhesus monkeys are normally distributed with
a mean of 17 pounds and a standard deviation of 3 pounds. What is the probability
that a randomly selected adult male rhesus monkey has a weight less than
14 pounds?

In Exercises 19 and 20, use the following information.

Apples The annual per person consumption of apples in the United States is normally
distributed with a mean of 16 pounds and a standard deviation of 4 pounds.

19. Find the *z*-score for an annual per person consumption of 22 pounds.

20. What is the probability that a randomly selected person in the United States has an
annual per person consumption of apples less than 22 pounds?

LESSON 11.4 Practice
For use with pages 766–771

Identify the type of sample described. Then tell if the sample is biased.
Explain **your reasoning.**

1. A consumer advocacy group wants to know if car owners believe their car is reliable. The group randomly selects 1020 car owners and mails out a survey to each one.

2. A grocery store wants to know which day of the week consumers prefer to do their grocery shopping. Everyone who shops at the store on Friday is asked which day of the week they prefer to do their grocery shopping.

3. A survey of students' favorite school subjects is being conducted. Every other student in the math club is asked "Which school subject is your favorite?"

Find the margin of error for a survey that has the given sample size.
Round your answer to the nearest tenth of a percent.

4. 200   **5.** 350   **6.** 1100   **7.** 2600

8. 5200   **9.** 495   **10.** 280   **11.** 9000

Find the sample size required to achieve the given margin of error.
Round your answer to the nearest whole number.

12. $\pm 2\%$ **13.** $\pm 4\%$ **14.** $\pm 9.5\%$ **15.** $\pm 2.7\%$

16. $\pm 4.5\%$ **17.** $\pm 0.5\%$ **18.** $\pm 3.6\%$ **19.** $\pm 7.5\%$

LESSON 11.4

Practice *continued*

For use with pages 766–771

In Exercises 20 and 21, use the following information.

Technology Survey In a survey of 504 people in the United States, about 11% said that the influx of new technologies such as computers has left them feeling overwhelmed.

20. What is the margin of error for the survey? Round your answer to the nearest tenth of a percent.

21. Give an interval that is likely to contain the exact percent of all people in the United States who feel overwhelmed by the influx of new technologies.

In Exercises 22–25, use the following information.

TV in the Bedroom A survey reported that 510 kids ages 8 to 18, or 68% of those surveyed, have a TV in their bedroom.

22. How many kids ages 8 to 18 were surveyed?

23. What is the margin of error for the survey? Round your answer to the nearest tenth of a percent.

24. Give an interval that is likely to contain the exact percent of all kids ages 8 to 18 who have a TV in their bedroom

25. About how many kids ages 8 to 18 should be surveyed to have a margin of error of 2.5%?

Practice
For use with pages 774–780

Determine which type of function best models the data points. Explain.

1.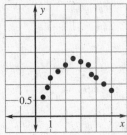

2.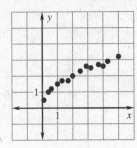

3.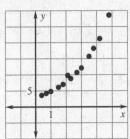

Determine the equation that best models the data.

4.

x	2	6	9	15	17	23	27
y	5	2	1	2	4	9	15

A. $y = 1.54x^{0.37}$

B. $y = 0.4x - 0.28$

C. $y = 0.05x^2 - 1.18x + 7.14$

D. $y = 1.44(1.07)^x$

Name _____   Date _____

LESSON 11.5

Practice *continued*
For use with pages 774–780

5.

x	2	5	7	10	13	15	19
y	24	14	10	6	4	3	1

A. $y = 35.3(0.84)^x$

B. $y = -1.24x + 21.48$

C. $y = 86.46x^{-1.27}$

D. $y = 0.095x^2 - 3.22x + 28.91$

6.

x	3	6	9	12	15	18	21	24
y	26	37	49	56	67	74	83	96

A. $y = 25.86(1.06)^x$

B. $y = 3.2x + 17.82$

C. $y = 12.63x^{0.62}$

D. $y = 0.01x^3 - 0.2x^2 + 5.6x + 10.4$

7. Black Bears The table shows the weight *w* (in kilograms) and the chest-girth circumference *c* (in centimeters) for 9 male black bears in West Virginia. Use the *regression* feature of a graphing calculator to find a function that models the data. What is the weight of a male black bear that has a chest-girth circumference of 119 centimeters?

w	82	90	101	112	125	136	144	152	160
c	91	94	99	103	108	112	116	119	122

Copyright © by McDougal Littell, a division of Houghton Mifflin Company.

Algebra 2
170 Chapter 11 Practice Workbook

 **Practice**
For use with pages 794–801

Write the first six terms of the sequence.

1. $a_n = n^2 + 6$

2. $a_n = n^2 - 3$

3. $a_n = 3^{n+1}$

4. $f(n) = 2^{n-1}$

5. $f(n) = -\dfrac{4}{3n}$

6. $f(n) = \dfrac{n}{3n + 2}$

For the sequence, describe the pattern, write the next term, and write a rule for the nth term.

7. $2, 4, 8, 16$

8. $1, 8, 27, 64$

9. $\dfrac{1}{1}, \dfrac{1}{4}, \dfrac{1}{9}, \dfrac{1}{16}$

10. $\dfrac{4}{3}, \dfrac{5}{3}, \dfrac{6}{3}, \dfrac{7}{3}$

11. $3, 5, 7, 9$

12. $\dfrac{4}{2}, \dfrac{8}{3}, \dfrac{12}{4}, \dfrac{16}{5}$

13. $0.7, 1.3, 1.9, 2.5$

14. $1.0, 0.5, 0.0, -0.5$

LESSON 12.1 **Practice** *continued*
For use with pages 794–801

Graph the sequence.

15. 1, 2, 3, 4, 5

16. 2, 4, 6, 8, 10

17. $\frac{1}{2}, 1, \frac{3}{2}, 2, \frac{5}{2}$

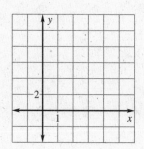
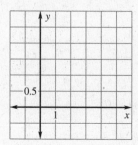

Write the series using summation notation.

18. $-2 + 1 + 6 + 13 + 22 + \cdots$

19. $\frac{2}{3} + \frac{4}{5} + \frac{6}{6} + \frac{8}{7}$

Find the sum of the series.

20. $\displaystyle\sum_{k=4}^{8} 3k - 2$

21. $\displaystyle\sum_{i=2}^{4} i^2 + i + 4$

22. $\displaystyle\sum_{i=1}^{22} i$

23. Jacket You want to save $30 to buy a jacket. You begin by saving a dollar in the first week. You plan to save an additional dollar each week after that. For example, you will save $2 in the second week, $3 in the third week, and so on. How many weeks must you save to have saved $30?

Name _____ Date _____

Tell whether the sequence is arithmetic. *Explain* why or why not.

1. $2, -5, -12, -19, -26$ **2.** $3, 5.5, 8, 10.5, 13$ **3.** $0, -5, -10, -12, -20$

4. $2, 4, 8, 16, 32$ **5.** $1, 2, 4, 7, 11$ **6.** $\dfrac{3}{4}, \dfrac{7}{8}, 1, \dfrac{9}{8}, \dfrac{5}{4}$

Write a rule for the *n*th term of the arithmetic sequence. Then find a_{10}.

7. $-4, 2, 8, 14, 20$ **8.** $-25, -29, -33, -37, -41$

9. $\dfrac{1}{4}, 0, -\dfrac{1}{4}, -\dfrac{1}{2}, -\dfrac{3}{4}$ **10.** $d = 5, a_5 = 33$

11. $d = 2, a_6 = 10$ **12.** $d = -3, a_{12} = -34.5$

Write a rule for the *n*th term of the arithmetic sequence that has the two given terms.

13. $a_{20} = 240, a_{15} = 170$ **14.** $a_6 = 13, a_{14} = 25$ **15.** $a_9 = -14, a_{15} = -20$

16. $a_8 = -44, a_5 = -32$ **17.** $a_{16} = 6, a_{20} = 7$ **18.** $a_7 = \dfrac{6}{7}, a_9 = \dfrac{2}{3}$

Practice *continued*
For use with pages 802–809

Find the sum of the arithmetic series.

19. $\displaystyle\sum_{i=1}^{8}(3i-1)$

20. $\displaystyle\sum_{i=1}^{20}(-2i+14)$

21. $\displaystyle\sum_{i=1}^{15}(-i-6)$

22. $\displaystyle\sum_{i=6}^{12}(-5i+17)$

23. $\displaystyle\sum_{i=4}^{9}(6i-30)$

24. $\displaystyle\sum_{i=8}^{16}(-11+4i)$

Write a rule for the sequence whose graph is shown.

25.
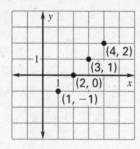

26.
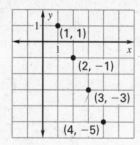

27.
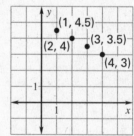

28. Auditorium An auditorium has 25 rows. The first row has 10 seats, and each row after the first has 1 more seat that the row before it.

a. Write a rule for the number of seats in the nth row.

b. Find the total number of seats in the auditorium.

LESSON 12.3 Practice
For use with pages 810–817

Tell whether the sequence is geometric. *Explain* why or why not.

1. $3, 5, 7, 9, 11, \ldots$

2. $5, 10, 20, 40, 80, \ldots$

3. $100, 50, 25, \dfrac{25}{2}, \dfrac{25}{4}, \ldots$

4. $1, 3, 7, 15, 31, \ldots$

5. $3, 9, 27, 81, 243, \ldots$

6. $-6, -2, -\dfrac{2}{3}, -\dfrac{2}{9}, -\dfrac{2}{27}, \ldots$

Write a rule for the *n*th term of the geometric sequence. Find a_6. Then graph the first five terms of the sequence.

7. $r = 3, a_1 = 2$

8. $r = \dfrac{1}{10}, a_2 = 4$

9. $r = -\dfrac{1}{2}, a_3 = 8$

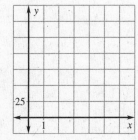
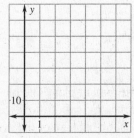
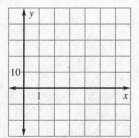

Write a rule for the *n*th term of the geometric sequence that has the two given terms.

10. $a_1 = 1, a_3 = 9$

11. $a_3 = 24, a_5 = 96$

12. $a_2 = 2, a_6 = 512$

13. $a_2 = 2, a_5 = \dfrac{1}{4}$

14. $a_3 = 25, a_6 = -\dfrac{25}{64}$

15. $a_4 = -\dfrac{8}{9}, a_7 = -\dfrac{64}{243}$

Find the sum of the geometric series.

16. $\displaystyle\sum_{i=1}^{5} 3(2)^{i-1}$

17. $\displaystyle\sum_{i=1}^{8} 90\left(\dfrac{1}{3}\right)^{i-1}$

18. $\displaystyle\sum_{i=1}^{10} 32\left(\dfrac{1}{2}\right)^{i-1}$

19. $\displaystyle\sum_{i=1}^{10} 8(3)^{i-1}$

20. $\displaystyle\sum_{i=0}^{7} 2\left(\dfrac{3}{2}\right)^{i-1}$

21. $\displaystyle\sum_{i=0}^{10} 1000\left(\dfrac{1}{2}\right)^{i-1}$

22. **Retirement** You invest \$20,000 in a retirement plan. The plan is expected to have an annual return of 12%. Write a rule for the amount of money a_n available in the plan at the beginning of the *n*th year. What is the balance of the account at the beginning of the 20th year?

LESSON 12.4 **Practice**
For use with pages 819–825

For the given series, find and graph the partial sums S_n for $n = 1, 2, 3, 4,$ and 5. *Describe* what happens to S_n as n increases.

1. $1 + \dfrac{1}{2} + \dfrac{1}{4} + \dfrac{1}{8} + \dfrac{1}{16} + \cdots$

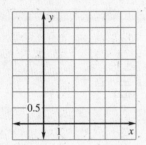

2. $3 + \dfrac{3}{4} + \dfrac{3}{16} + \dfrac{3}{64} + \dfrac{3}{256} + \cdots$

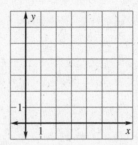

Find the sum of the infinite geometric series, if it exists.

3. $\displaystyle\sum_{i=1}^{\infty} 5\left(\dfrac{1}{2}\right)^{i-1}$

4. $\displaystyle\sum_{i=1}^{\infty} \left(\dfrac{1}{5}\right)^{i-1}$

5. $\displaystyle\sum_{i=1}^{\infty} 3\left(-\dfrac{2}{5}\right)^{i-1}$

6. $\displaystyle\sum_{i=0}^{\infty} 2(6)^{i-1}$

7. $\displaystyle\sum_{i=1}^{\infty} 6\left(\dfrac{2}{3}\right)^{i-1}$

8. $\displaystyle\sum_{i=1}^{\infty} 8\left(\dfrac{1}{3}\right)^{i-1}$

9. $\displaystyle\sum_{i=1}^{\infty} \left(\dfrac{5}{2}\right)^{i-1}$

10. $\displaystyle\sum_{i=0}^{\infty} 2\left(-\dfrac{3}{4}\right)^{i}$

11. $\displaystyle\sum_{i=0}^{\infty} 7\left(\dfrac{4}{7}\right)^{i}$

LESSON
12.4
Practice *continued*
For use with pages 819–825

Find the sum of the infinite geometric series, if it exists.

12. $2 + \dfrac{2}{3} + \dfrac{2}{9} + \dfrac{2}{27} + \dfrac{2}{81} + \cdots$

13. $\dfrac{1}{3} + \dfrac{1}{4} + \dfrac{3}{16} + \dfrac{9}{64} + \dfrac{27}{256} + \cdots$

14. $\dfrac{1}{2} + \dfrac{3}{4} + \dfrac{9}{8} + \dfrac{27}{16} + \dfrac{81}{32} + \cdots$

15. $\dfrac{2}{3} + \dfrac{2}{5} + \dfrac{6}{25} + \dfrac{18}{125} + \dfrac{54}{625} + \cdots$

Write the repeating decimal as a fraction in lowest terms.

16. $0.555\ldots$

17. $0.262626\ldots$

18. $0.538538538\ldots$

19. $17.171717\ldots$

20. $311.311311311\ldots$

21. $0.040404\ldots$

22. **Retirement** You invest $15,000 in a retirement plan. The plan is expected to have an annual return of 9%. Write a rule for the amount of money a_n available in the plan at the beginning of the nth year. What is the balance of the account at the beginning of the 25th year?

23. **Ball Bounce** A ball is dropped from a height of 40 feet. Each time it hits the ground, it bounces three-fourths of its previous height. Find the total distance the ball has traveled before coming to rest.

Practice
LESSON 12.5 *For use with pages 826–833*

Write the first five terms of the sequence.

1. $a_0 = 3$

$a_n = a_{n-1} + 7$

2. $a_0 = -4$

$a_n = 2a_{n-1}$

3. $a_0 = 243$

$a_n = \frac{1}{3}a_{n-1} + 9$

4. $a_0 = 2$

$a_n = n^2 - 3n + 2a_{n-1}$

5. $a_0 = 2$

$a_n = (a_{n-1})^2 - 3$

6. $a_1 = 3, a_2 = 1$

$a_n = a_{n-1} - a_{n-2}$

Write a recursive rule for the sequence. The sequence may be arithmetic, geometric, or neither.

7. 2, 4, 6, 8, 10, . . .

8. 6, 10, 14, 18, 22, . . .

9. 2, 6, 18, 54, 162, . . .

10. −3, 15, −75, 375, −1875, . . .

11. 10, 4, −2, −8, −14, . . .

12. 32, 16, 8, 4, 2, . . .

13. 1, 3, 4, 7, 11, . . .

14. 2, 4, 16, 256, 65536, . . .

LESSON
12.5

Practice *continued*
For use with pages 826–833

Find the first three iterates of the function for the given initial value.

15. $f(x) = x + 2, x_0 = 0$ **16.** $f(x) = x - 3, x_0 = 12$

17. $f(x) = 2x - 6, x_0 = 4$ **18.** $f(x) = 4x + 5, x_0 = 3$

19. $f(x) = -3x + 2, x_0 = -2$ **20.** $f(x) = x^2 + 3, x_0 = 1$

21. $f(x) = \frac{1}{2}x^2 - 4, x_0 = 6$ **22.** $f(x) = x^2 - x - 2, x_0 = 2$

In Exercises 23–25, use the following information.

Tree Farm A tree farm initially has 5000 trees. Each year 10% of the trees are harvested and 450 seedlings are planted.

23. Write a recursive rule for the number of trees on the tree farm at the beginning of the nth year.

24. How many trees remain at the beginning of the fifth year?

25. What happens to the tree population over time?

In Exercises 26 and 27, use the following information.

Savings Account On January 1, 2006, you have $500 in a savings account which earns 0.25% per month. On the last day of every month you deposit $80.

26. Write a recursive rule for the account balance at the beginning of the nth month.

27. Assuming you do not withdraw any money from the account, what will the balance be on August 1, 2006?

Name _____ Date _____

Evaluate the six trigonometric functions of the angle θ.

1.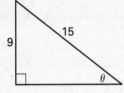

2.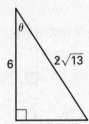

Let θ be an acute angle of a right triangle. Find the values of the other five trigonometric functions of θ.

3. $\sin \theta = \dfrac{4}{5}$

4. $\cos \theta = \dfrac{5}{6}$

5. $\sec \theta = \dfrac{\sqrt{73}}{8}$

6. $\cot \theta = \sqrt{3}$

Find the exact values of x and y.

7.

8.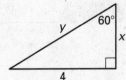

9.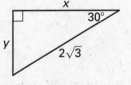

LESSON 13.1   **Practice** *continued*
For use with pages 852–858

Solve △DEF using the diagram and the given measurements.

10. $D = 40°, f = 8$

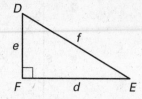

11. $E = 53°, d = 13$

12. $D = 67°, e = 10.5$

13. **Shadow** A person casts the shadow shown. What is the approximate height of the person?

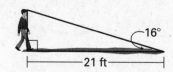

14. **Mountains** A hiker at the top of a mountain sees a farm and an airport in the distance.

a. What is the distance d from the hiker to the farm?

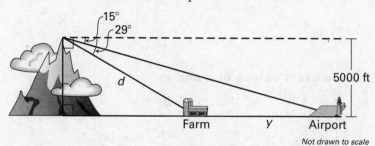

Not drawn to scale

b. What is the distance y from the farm to the airport?

Name _____ Date _____

LESSON 13.2 Practice
For use with pages 859–865

Draw an angle with the given measure in standard position.

1. $130°$

2. $\dfrac{5\pi}{4}$

3. $-\dfrac{2\pi}{3}$

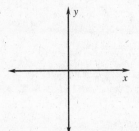

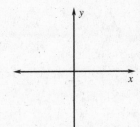

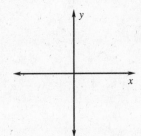

Find one positive angle and one negative angle that are coterminal with the given angle.

4. $-35°$

5. $280°$

6. $-\dfrac{\pi}{6}$

7. $\dfrac{7\pi}{5}$

Convert the degree measure to radians or the radian measure to degrees.

8. $270°$

9. $-135°$

10. $\dfrac{11\pi}{6}$

11. $-\dfrac{\pi}{18}$

Name _____   Date _____

**Find the arc length and area of a sector with the given radius *r* and
central angle *θ*.**

12. $r = 5$ m, $\theta = \dfrac{\pi}{2}$
13. $r = 7$ in., $\theta = \dfrac{3\pi}{4}$
14. $r = 11$ ft, $\theta = 200°$

**Evaluate the trigonometric function using a calculator if necessary.
If possible, give an exact answer.**

15. $\cos \dfrac{\pi}{4}$
16. $\sin \dfrac{\pi}{6}$
17. $\cot \dfrac{\pi}{9}$
18. $\csc \dfrac{4\pi}{5}$

19. Swing At an amusement park, you ride a swing that takes you
several revolutions counterclockwise as shown in the diagram.
Find the measure of the angle generated as you are on the ride.
Give the answer in both degrees and radians.

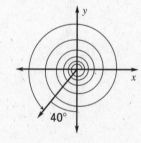

20. Cheese A circular piece of cheese has a portion cut out as shown.

a. What is the approximate arc length of the portion that is missing?

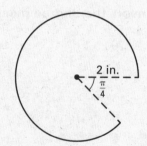

b. What is the approximate area of the portion that is missing?

Name _____ Date _____

Practice
For use with pages 866–872

Use the given point on the terminal side of an angle θ **in standard position to evaluate the six trigonometric functions of** θ.

1. $(8, -15)$

2. $(-7, -2)$

Evaluate the six trigonometric functions of θ.

3. $\theta = 90°$

4. $\theta = -\pi$

Sketch the angle. Then find its reference angle.

5. $-115°$

6. $125°$

7. $325°$

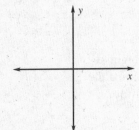
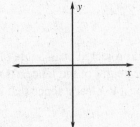
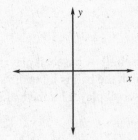

8. $-\dfrac{17\pi}{6}$

9. $-\dfrac{7\pi}{4}$

10. $\dfrac{11\pi}{3}$

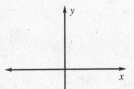
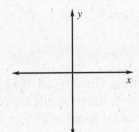
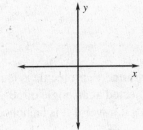

LESSON 13.3 **Practice** *continued*
For use with pages 866–872

Evaluate the function without using a calculator.

11. $\sin 240°$ **12.** $\tan 150°$ **13.** $\sec(-315°)$ **14.** $\cot(-150°)$

15. $\cos\left(-\dfrac{3\pi}{4}\right)$ **16.** $\csc \dfrac{7\pi}{6}$ **17.** $\tan \dfrac{8\pi}{3}$ **18.** $\sin\left(-\dfrac{5\pi}{6}\right)$

19. Distance A projectile is launched with an initial speed of 42 feet per second. It is projected at an angle of 50°. How far does the projectile travel? How much farther does it travel if it is launched with an initial speed of 84 feet per second?

20. Baseball A baseball player hits a ball projected at an angle of 40°. The height at which the ball is hit is the same as the height of the fence. At what speed must the baseball player hit the ball in order for it to clear a fence that is 385 feet away?

Name _____ Date _____

 **LESSON 13.4** **Practice**
For use with pages 874–880

Evaluate the expression without using a calculator. Give your answer in both radians and degrees.

1. $\cos^{-1}(-1)$

2. $\tan^{-1}\dfrac{\sqrt{3}}{3}$

3. $\sin^{-1} 0$

4. $\sin^{-1}\left(-\dfrac{\sqrt{2}}{2}\right)$

5. $\tan^{-1} 1$

6. $\cos^{-1} 2$

Use a calculator to evaluate the expression in both radians and degrees.

7. $\tan^{-1}(-1.7)$

8. $\cos^{-1} 0.24$

9. $\sin^{-1} 0.85$

10. $\tan^{-1}(4.1)$

11. $\sin^{-1}(-0.99)$

12. $\cos^{-1}(-0.1)$

Solve the equation for θ.

13. $\sin \theta = -0.71;\ 270° < \theta < 360°$

14. $\tan \theta = 1.6;\ 180° < \theta < 270°$

15. $\cos \theta = 0.22;\ 270° < \theta < 360°$

16. $\cos \theta = -0.22;\ 180° < \theta < 270°$

Name _____ Date _____

Find the measure of the angle θ.

17.

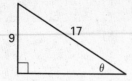

18.

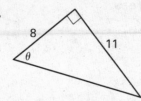

19.

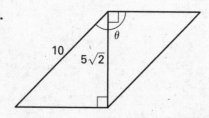

20. **Carpentry** You are making a door stopper from a block of wood. When the door rests against the stopper, you want the corner of the stopper to extend through the width of the door. If the bottom of the 1.7-inch wide door is 0.7 inch off the ground, what is the angle θ of the door stopper?

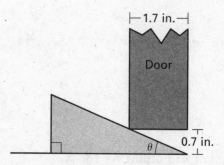

21. **Flight** A falcon perched at a height of 100 feet descends straight toward a prey that is 125 feet away. At what angle does it descend? If the falcon ascends along the same path as it descended, at what angle does it ascend?

Name _____ Date _____

LESSON 13.5 **Practice**
For use with pages 881–888

Solve △ABC.

1.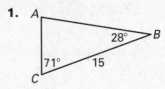

2.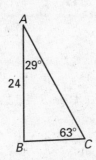

3.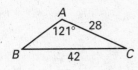

Solve △ABC. (*Hint:* Some of the "triangles" have no solution and some have two solutions.)

4. $A = 72°, B = 35°, c = 21$

5. $A = 95°, C = 35°, c = 18$

6. $A = 105°, a = 11, b = 13$

7. $B = 10°, C = 23°, a = 15$

8. $A = 60°, B = 32°, b = 26$

9. $C = 49°, a = 24, c = 19$

LESSON 13.5 **Practice** *continued*
For use with pages 881–888

Find the area of △ABC.

10. $B = 141°, a = 7, c = 8$

11. $C = 70°, a = 30, b = 24$

12. $A = 99°, b = 20, c = 27$

13. $B = 32°, a = 18, c = 13$

14.

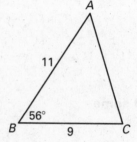

15.

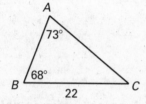

16.

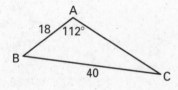

17. Utility Poles After a storm, two street lights with the same length are leaning against each other. The bases of the poles are 45 feet apart. The angles that the poles make with the ground are 50° and 60°. Using the diagram shown at the right, find c.

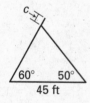

18. Maps The state of New Hampshire is approximately triangular in shape. Use the diagram shown at the right to estimate the area of the state to the nearest thousand square miles.

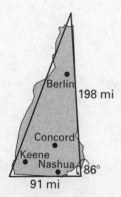

Practice
LESSON 13.6
For use with pages 889–894

Solve △ ABC.

1.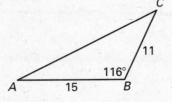

2.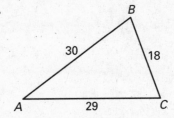

3. $a = 12, b = 13, c = 20$

4. $B = 135°, a = 19, c = 7$

5. $A = 46°, b = 24, c = 10$

6. $C = 3°, a = 16, b = 33$

7. $a = 17, b = 37, c = 23$

8. $a = 42, b = 43, c = 38$

Find the area of △ ABC.

9.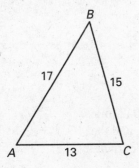

10.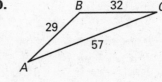

LESSON 13.6 **Practice** *continued*
For use with pages 889–894

11. $a = 6, b = 8, c = 12$ **12.** $a = 15, b = 10, c = 9$

13. $a = 20, b = 25, c = 14$ **14.** $a = 32, b = 37, c = 7$

15. $a = 55, b = 50, c = 42$ **16.** $a = 38, b = 50, c = 72$

17. **Flagpole** A 5-foot long flagpole that is angled on the side of a building is casting a 3 foot long shadow. The distance from the end of the flagpole to the end of the shadow is 4.1 feet. Use the diagram to find θ.

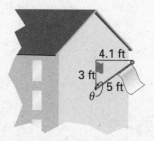

18. **Distance** The distance between Miami, Florida and Bermuda is about 1042 miles. The distance from Bermuda to San Juan, Puerto Rico is about 965 miles, and the distance from San Juan to Miami is about 1038 miles. Find the area of the triangle formed by the three locations.

LESSON 14.1 Practice

For use with pages 908–914

Match the function with its graph.

1. $y = 3 \sin 2x$

2. $y = 3 \sin \frac{1}{2}x$

3. $y = 3 \cos 2x$

A.

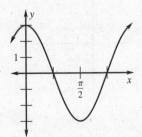

B.

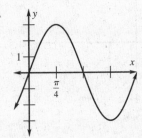

C.

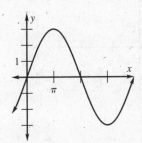

Graph one cycle of the function. Identify the amplitude and period.

4. $y = 5 \tan 3x$

5. $y = 3 \cos \frac{2}{3}x$

6. $y = \pi \sin 2x$

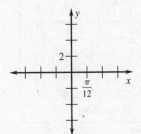

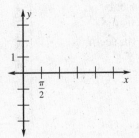

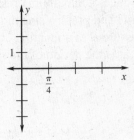

Practice *continued*
For use with pages 908–914

7. $y = \dfrac{1}{2} \cos 3\pi x$

8. $y = 2 \sin \pi x$

9. $y = 3 \tan \dfrac{1}{3}\pi x$

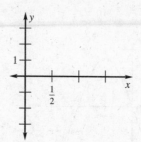

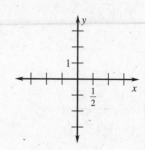

10. Tuning Forks A tuning fork vibrates with a frequency of 220 hertz (cycles per second). You strike the tuning fork with a force that produces a maximum pressure of 3 pascals. Write and graph a sine model that gives the pressure P as a function of the time t (in seconds). What is the period of the sound wave?

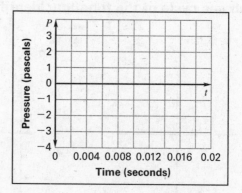

LESSON 14.2 **Practice**
For use with pages 915–922

Graph the function.

1. $y = -\sin\left(x - \frac{\pi}{3}\right) - 3$

2. $y = -\tan\left(x + \frac{\pi}{2}\right) - 2$

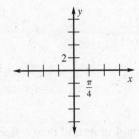

3. $y = 2 - \cos(2x + \pi)$

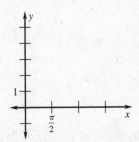

4. $y = 1 - \tan\left(x - \frac{\pi}{4}\right)$

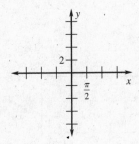

5. $y = 3 - \cos\left(x + \frac{3\pi}{2}\right)$

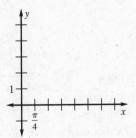

6. $y = -\frac{1}{2}\sin(2x + 3\pi)$

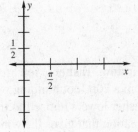

LESSON 14.2 **Practice** *continued*
For use with pages 915–922

Write an equation of the graph described.

7. The graph of $y = -2 \tan 5x$ translated down 4 units and left π units

8. The graph of $y = \frac{1}{4} \cos 2x$ translated up 4 units and then reflected in the x-axis

9. The graph of $y = \frac{1}{2} \sin 4x$ translated right 3 units and then reflected in the line $y = -2$

10. **Window Washers** You are standing 70 feet from a 200 foot building, watching as a window washer lowers himself to the ground. Write an equation that gives the window washer's distance d (in feet) from the top of the building as a function of the angle of elevation θ. State the domain of the function. Then graph the function. What is the angle of elevation if the window washer has lowered himself halfway down the building?

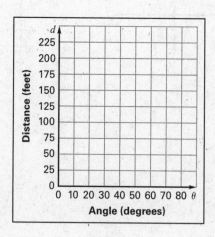

Name _____ Date _____

 Practice
14.3 *For use with pages 923–930*

Find the values of the other five trigonometric functions of θ.

1. $\sin \theta = -\dfrac{15}{17}, \ \pi < \theta < \dfrac{3\pi}{2}$

2. $\tan \theta = \dfrac{3}{4}, \ 0 < \theta < \dfrac{\pi}{2}$

3. $\cos \theta = -\dfrac{1}{2}, \ \dfrac{\pi}{2} < \theta < \pi$

4. $\sec \theta = \sqrt{5}, \ \dfrac{3\pi}{2} < \theta < 2\pi$

Simplify the expression.

5. $\sec(-x)\cot(-x)\sin(-x)$

6. $\dfrac{\cos^2 x}{\sin x} + \sin x$

7. $\dfrac{1 - \cos^2 x}{\cos^2 x}$

8. $\sin^3 x + \cos\left(\dfrac{\pi}{2} - x\right)\cos^2 x$

9. $\csc(-x) - \csc(-x)\cos^2 x$

10. $\dfrac{1 + \sec(-x)}{\sin(-x) + \tan(-x)}$

LESSON 14.3 **Practice** *continued*
For use with pages 915–922

Verify the identity.

11. $\cos x \sec x = 1$

12. $1 - \tan^2 x = 2 - \sec^2 x$

13. $\dfrac{\tan^2 x}{\sec x} = \sec x - \cos x$

14. $\tan\left(\dfrac{\pi}{2} - x\right) \sin x = \cos x$

15. $\dfrac{\cos^2 x}{1 + \tan^2 x} + \dfrac{\sin^2 x}{\sec^2 x} = \cos^2 x$

16. $\dfrac{\sin\left(\dfrac{\pi}{2} - x\right) - 1}{1 - \cos(-x)} = -1$

17. Rate of Change In calculus, it can be shown that the rate of change of the function
$f(x) = \sec x \cot x$ is given by the expression:

$-\csc^2 x \sec x + \cot x \sec x \tan x.$

Show that this expression for the rate of change can be written as $-\csc x \cot x$.

18. Using Identities Use the cotangent identity to describe what happens to the value
of $\cot \theta$ as the value of $\cos \theta$ decreases and the value of $\sin \theta$ increases. On what
intervals does this happen?

LESSON 14.4 **Practice**
For use with pages 931–937

Find the general solution of the equation.

1. $\sqrt{2}\cos x - 1 = 0$

2. $7\sec x - 7 = 0$

3. $5\cos x - \sqrt{3} = 3\cos x$

4. $\csc x - 2 = 0$

Solve the equation in the interval $0 \le x < 2\pi$.

5. $2\cot^4 x - \cot^2 x - 15 = 0$

6. $2\sin^4 x - \sin^2 x = 0$

7. $2\csc x + 17 = 15 + \csc x$

8. $\sec x \csc x - 2\csc x = 0$

9. $3\tan^3 x - \tan x = 0$

10. $\cos x \csc^2 x + 3\cos x = 7\cos x$

11. $\sqrt{2}\cos x \sin x - \cos x = 0$

12. $3\sec^2 x - 4 = 0$

13. **Approximate Solutions** Use a graphing calculator to approximate the solutions of $3 \tan^2 2x = 1$ in the interval $0 \le x < \pi$. Round your answer to two decimal places.

14. **Find Points of Intersection** Find the points of intersection of the graphs of the given functions in the interval $0 \le x < 2\pi$.

$y = \sin x \tan x$

$y = 2 - \cos x$

15. **Calculus** In calculus, it can be shown that the function $y = 2 \sin x - \cos 2x$ has minimum and maximum values when $2 \cos x + 4 \cos x \sin x = 0$. Find all solutions of $2 \cos x + 4 \cos x \sin x = 0$ in the interval $0 \le x < 2\pi$. Verify your solutions with a graphing calculator.

In Exercises 16 and 17, use the following information.

Area The area A of a rectangle inscribed in one arch of the graph of $y = \cos x$ is given by $A = 2x \cos x$ for $0 \le x \le \dfrac{\pi}{2}$.

16. Use a graphing utility to graph the area function and approximate the area of the largest inscribed rectangle.

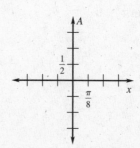

17. Determine the values of x for which $A \ge 1$.

LESSON 14.5 **Practice**
For use with pages 941–948

Write a function for the sinusoid.

1.
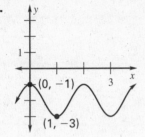
$(0, -1)$
3
$(1, -3)$

2.
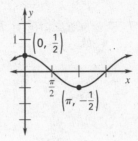
$\left(0, \frac{1}{2}\right)$
$\frac{\pi}{2}$
$\left(\pi, -\frac{1}{2}\right)$

3.
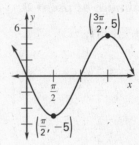
6
$\left(\frac{3\pi}{2}, 5\right)$
$\frac{\pi}{2}$
$\left(\frac{\pi}{2}, -5\right)$

4.
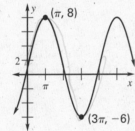
$(\pi, 8)$
2
π
$(3\pi, -6)$

5.
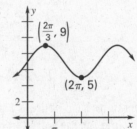
$\left(\frac{2\pi}{3}, 9\right)$
$(2\pi, 5)$
2
π

6.
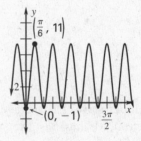
$\left(\frac{\pi}{6}, 11\right)$
2
$(0, -1)$
$\frac{3\pi}{2}$

LESSON 14.5 **Practice** *continued*
For use with pages 941–948

Write a trigonometric function for the sinusoid with maximum at point _A_ and minimum at point _B_.

7. $A(3, 7), B(1, -3)$

8. $A(0, 3), B(2\pi, -3)$

9. $A(0.5, 5), B(1.5, -15)$

10. $A\left(\frac{1}{4}, 2\right), B\left(\frac{3}{4}, 0\right)$

11. $A\left(\frac{\pi}{3}, 4\right), B(0, 2)$

12. $A(9\pi, 1), B(3\pi, -5)$

13. **Temperature** The average daily temperature T (in degrees Fahrenheit) in Detroit, Michigan is given in the table. Time t is measured in months, with $t = 0$ representing January 1. Use a graphing calculator to write a sinusoidal model that gives T as a function of t.

t	0.5	1.5	2.5	3.5	4.5	5.5
T	24.5	27.2	36.9	48.1	59.8	69.0

t	6.5	7.5	8.5	9.5	10.5	11.5
T	73.5	71.8	63.9	51.9	40.7	29.6

Name _____ Date _____

Find the exact value of the expression.

1. $\cos 105°$ **2.** $\sin 195°$ **3.** $\tan 165°$

4. $\tan \dfrac{\pi}{12}$ **5.** $\sec \dfrac{19\pi}{12}$ **6.** $\sin \dfrac{13\pi}{12}$

Evaluate the expression given $\cos u = \dfrac{4}{5}$ with $0 < u < \dfrac{\pi}{2}$ and $\tan v = \dfrac{8}{15}$ with $\pi < v < \dfrac{3\pi}{2}$.

7. $\sin(u + v)$ **8.** $\cos(u + v)$ **9.** $\tan(u + v)$

10. $\sin(u - v)$ **11.** $\cos(u - v)$ **12.** $\tan(u - v)$

Simplify, but do *not* evaluate, the expression.

13. $\sin 20° \cos 50° + \cos 20° \sin 50°$ **14.** $\cos \dfrac{\pi}{4} \cos \dfrac{\pi}{3} - \sin \dfrac{\pi}{4} \sin \dfrac{\pi}{3}$

15. $\dfrac{\tan 68° - \tan 54°}{1 + \tan 68° \tan 54°}$ **16.** $\dfrac{1 - \tan \dfrac{5\pi}{3} \tan \dfrac{\pi}{4}}{\tan \dfrac{5\pi}{3} + \tan \dfrac{\pi}{4}}$

LESSON 14.6

Practice *continued*

For use with pages 949–954

Solve the equation for $0 \leq x < 2\pi$.

17. $\cos\left(x + \dfrac{\pi}{4}\right) - \cos\left(x - \dfrac{\pi}{4}\right) = 1$

18. $\sin\left(x + \dfrac{\pi}{6}\right) - \sin\left(x - \dfrac{\pi}{6}\right) = \dfrac{1}{2}$

19. $\tan(x + \pi) + \cos\left(x - \dfrac{\pi}{2}\right) = 0$

20. $\sin(x + \pi) + \sin(x - \pi) = 2$

In Exercises 21 and 22, use the following information.

Geometry In the figure shown, the acute angle of intersection, $\theta_2 - \theta_1$, of two lines with slopes m_1 and m_2 is given by

$$\tan(\theta_2 - \theta_1) = \dfrac{m_2 - m_1}{1 + m_1 m_2}.$$

21. Find the acute angle of intersection of the lines

$y = \dfrac{1}{4}x - 2$ and $y = 4x + 5$.

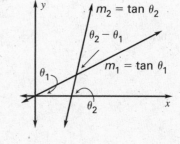

22. Find the acute angle of intersection of the lines $y = x + 2$ and $y = 3x + 2$.

Practice
For use with pages 955–962

Find the exact value of the expression.

1. $\tan 67.5°$

2. $\sin \dfrac{5\pi}{8}$

3. $\cos \dfrac{3\pi}{8}$

Find the exact values of $\sin \dfrac{u}{2}$, $\cos \dfrac{u}{2}$, and $\tan \dfrac{u}{2}$.

4. $\tan u = \dfrac{3}{4}$, $\pi < u < \dfrac{3\pi}{2}$

5. $\sin u = -\dfrac{5}{13}$, $\dfrac{3\pi}{2} < u < 2\pi$

Find the exact values of $\sin 2x$, $\cos 2x$, and $\tan 2x$.

6. $\cos x = \dfrac{12}{13}$, $0 < x < \dfrac{\pi}{2}$

7. $\sin x = -\dfrac{4}{5}$, $\dfrac{3\pi}{2} < x < 2\pi$

Rewrite the expression without double angles or half angles, given that $0 < x < \dfrac{\pi}{2}$. Then simplify the expression.

8. $2 \csc 2x$

9. $\dfrac{\sin \frac{x}{2} \tan \frac{x}{2}}{1 - \cos x}$

10. $\dfrac{1 + \cos 2x}{\cot x}$

LESSON 14.7 **Practice** *continued*
For use with pages 955–962

Verify the identity.

11. $\cos 4x = 8 \cos^4 x - 8 \cos^2 x + 1$

12. $4 \sin \dfrac{x}{2} \cos \dfrac{x}{2} = 2 \sin x$

13. $(\sin x + \cos x)^2 = 1 + \sin 2x$

14. $\cos 3x = 4 \cos^3 x - 3 \cos x$

Solve the equation for $0 \le x < 2\pi$.

15. $\sec 2x = 2$ **16.** $\cos 2x = \cos x$ **17.** $\sin 2x \sin x = \cos x$

18. **Calculus** A graph of $y = \cos 2x + 2 \cos x$ in the interval $0 \le x < 2\pi$ is shown in the figure. In calculus, it can be shown that the function $y = \cos 2x + 2 \cos x$ has turning points when $\sin 2x + \sin x = 0$. Find the coordinates of these turning points.

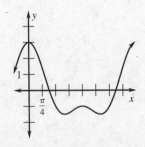